A Guide to Astrology for Lesbians

HerScopes

charlene lichtenstein

A Fireside Book
Published by Simon & Schuster
New York * London * Toronto * Sydney * Singapore

FIRESIDE
Rockefeller Center
1230 Avenue of the Americas
New York, NY 10020

FIRESIDE and colophon are registered trademarks
of Simon & Schuster, Inc.

Designed by Snap-Haus Graphics

Manufactured in the United States of America

1   3   5   7   9   10   8   6   4   2

Library of Congress Cataloging-in-Publication Data
Lichtenstein, Charlene.
Herscopes: a guide to astrology for lesbians / Charlene Lichtenstein.
p.   cm.
"A Fireside book."
1. Astrology and homosexuality.   2. Lesbians—Miscellanea.   I. Title.
BF1729.H66 L53 2000
133.5'086'643—dc21   00-023242

ISBN 0-684-86867-9

Acknowledgments

I would like to express my gratitude to the people who helped make this book possible. First, to Carrie Thornton at Simon & Schuster who approached me with the idea for the book. She has been a strong supporter throughout the entire process and a source of inspiration and strength. My appreciation to you is enormous.

Were it not for Clark at AccessNewAge, I might not have followed up on the book proposal. In his own soft spoken way (ha!) he encouraged me to pursue the project and has continued to be a booster as well as a discerning critic. My respect for your opinion is unwavering.

To my family and friends: When I was worried that I wouldn't have enough to say to fill a book, they assured me that, as usual, I would have more than enough to say, even if it wasn't all useful, logical or interesting. My world would be incomplete without all of you.

And I want to thank perhaps the most important person of all, Rickie, my Taurean Bull, who possesses all the patience of the earth signs, who nurtured me through periods of writer's block, who fed me and did not leave me while I retreated and wrote. My love for you knows no bounds.

Information for this book was culled from the following:

The Stonewall horoscope was computed on Matrix Software,

407 N. State Street, Big Rapids, MI 49307. The Stonewall quote is from *Stonewall* by Martin Duberman, Plume Press, 1994.

Quotes and birthdays were selected from various books and websites. Some of these include www.zodiacal.com, www.adze.com, www.famousbirthdays.com, www.astropro.com, A Word A Day e-mail and *The Secret Language of Birthdays* by Gary Goldschneider and Joost Elffers, published through the Penguin Group, 1994.

National Council of Geocosmic Research conventions and classes, as well as *The Mountain Astrologer Magazine* are both invaluable educational resources.

Mythology: Timeless Tales of Gods and Heroes by Edith Hamilton, The New American Library, 1942. *The Age of Fable* by Thomas Bulfinch, E. P. Dutton & Co., 1906.

This book is dedicated to
my aunt Barbara, in blessed memory,
and to my parents

Contents

Introduction

*i don't believe in astrology; i'm a sagittarian
and we're skeptical.*
—sir arthur c. clarke

The come-on line that launched a thousand possibilities would have to be "Hey, babe, what's your sign?" I must admit that I have used that old trick a thousand times, but unlike some less discerning women, I always listen very carefully for the answer. After reading this book, you will too.

This handy-dandy volume of sun sign astrology is written expressly for women who love women but who also have to work, save money, grapple with personal challenges, deal with family and surly neighbors, welcome joy and prosperity, face defeat and awful bosses and perhaps even raise a brood of children who may change the world. It's for "fems," "butches," "lipstick lesbians," "drag kings," and women who refuse to be labeled (like those confounded Aquarians). Under all the exteriors, the lace and the leather, the buffed and the baggy, we are all the same, striving to make sense of our place in the world.

Here is fair warning: Sun sign astrology is a simplistic first-step approach to a complete astrological personality analysis. This book is full of blatantly crass generalizations as well as a few derogatory snippets thrown in for humorous effect. **Disclaimer: This book is for entertainment purposes only, so lighten up, girlfriend!** Let's face it, not all Aries are bullies, not all Taureans are stubborn and crude, not all Gemini are shallow and false, not all Cancers are moody, oversensitive whiners, not all Leos are overbearing and vain, not all Virgos are sniveling hypochondriacs, not all Libras are ineffective lightweights, not all Scorpios are deadly connivers, not all Sagittarians are clumsy louts with gross and disgusting table manners, not all Capricorns are morose corporate sellouts, not all Aquarians are cold-blooded opportunists and not all Pisces are using sychophants.

Some Aries are actually altruistic, mighty Aphrodite warriors, Taureans sensuous, cuddly bosom buddies, Gemini brilliant conversationalists, Cancers warm and nurturing full-bodied mamas, Leos generously gallant, Virgos sacrificing and magnanimous, Libras delightful, attractive companions, Scorpios zesty, experimental lovergrrls, Sagittarians jolly, fun-loving adventurers, Capricorns sentimental and forgiving compadres, "Aqueerians" all-giving, enlightened torch bearers and Pisces intuitive, romantic beauties. But do we ever get to meet them at the local dyke site? Probably not tonight, Irene!

A careful reading of *HerScopes* might very well teach you something valuable about yourself and your life. An added benefit: It can also reveal things about that mysterious babe you've been eyeing from across the produce counter. Go on, sister, ask her. . . . "What's your sign?"

your sun sign
Our sun sign is the most important component of our astrological chart and gives us insight into our basic personality. It is who we are and who we strive to be. It's the clothes we wear to give the world a glimpse of our personal style, preferences and tastes. Do we like to draw attention to ourselves? Are we prim and proper? Do we drape ourselves in haute couture while wearing underwear from before the flood? Obviously some of us are precise, unassuming, tasteful or bold and some of us are dreadful slobs (no names, please . . . Sagittarius!).

It's fairly common knowledge that there are twelve signs of the zodiac, but let's list them anyway.

sign	symbol	Birthdates
Aries	The Ram	March 21–April 19
Taurus	The Bull	April 20–May 20
Gemini	The Twins	May 21–June 21
Cancer	The Crab	June 22–July 22
Leo	The Lion	July 23–August 22
Virgo	The Virgin	August 23–September 22
Libra	The Scales	September 23–October 23
Scorpio	The Scorpion	October 24–November 22
Sagittarius	The Centaur	November 23–December 22
Capricorn	The Goat	December 23–January 20
Aquarius	The Water Carrier	January 21–February 19
Pisces	The Fish	February 20–March 20

For the benefit of those fatalistic Piscean fems who like to read volumes into every little Post-it Note and to satisfy your curiosity, 12 really is a rather mystical number. It should come as no surprise that there are:

    12 zodiacal signs
    12 months in a year
    12 tribes of Israel
    12 disciples of Christ
    12 inches in a foot
    12 items in a dozen
    12 times that you have to tell a Gemini to get her feet off the furniture . . . you get the idea.

Each sign is categorized by an *element* and a *mode*. Elements describe your state of being, whether you are a fire starter, full of hot air, all wet or solid like a rock. Modes indicate how tolerant of change you are or how much action you can take. I'll explain further.

There are four elements: fire, air, water and earth. Each sign is associated with one of these four elements. For example, fire signs are enthusiastic, energetic, extroverted, courageous and action oriented. They inspire others and heat up a room with their personal warmth. These zesty girlfriends are Aries, Leo and Sagittarius.

Air signs are intellectual, friendly, sociable and conceptually oriented but a bit removed in their approach to others. Don't try to probe their feelings; they ain't gonna let it happen. These charming yet logical women are Gemini, Libra and Aquarius.

Water signs are fluid, intuitive, comforting and emotionally oriented. They are the ones you want to cuddle with on a rainy night but avoid when the moon is full and they become Ms. Hydes. These introverted, sensitive babes are Cancer, Scorpio and Pisces.

Earth signs are no-nonsense, stable, purposeful, physical and process oriented. They really seem to care about what others think of them and are the first ones to help any galpal when her life turns to sludge. These practical girlfriends are Taurus, Virgo and Capricorn.

Old-time astrology books tend to match fire with air (air invigorates fire) and water with earth (water nourishes earth) but these are ridiculously wonky generalizations that will only prevent you from getting to know some pretty special gals a bit better.

Each sign also has its own mode. There are three of them: cardinal, mutable and fixed. Cardinal signs are pushy broads whose raison d'être is to create change, upend the landscape and move things along in whatever direction takes their fancy. They don't wait for the director to yell "action." They are action personified. Honey, you know the type. In case you were wondering, the Cardinal signs are Aries, Cancer, Libra and Capricorn.

Fixed signs are at the other end of the spectrum, resisting change or trying to solidify and create stasis around changing conditions. They are the ones who say, "Hold on a minute. Let's catch our breath and see where we are." They can be immovable like a rock, but like a rock, when they start to move, get out of the way! The fixed signs are Taurus, Leo, Scorpio and Aquarius.

Mutable signs are flexible souls, going with the flow and adapting to new challenges and situations. They are like the big oak that bends in the breeze but doesn't crack in half. The mutable signs are Gemini, Virgo, Sagittarius and Pisces.

Each sign has its own particular combination of element and mode. For example, the only fire/cardinal sign is Aries and the only fixed/water sign is Scorpio. Therefore, it is easy to get a thumbnail sketch of any alluring siren at the bar by simply checking the chart below. Consider this your quick cheat sheet as you buy her another drink and delve deeper.

sign	element	mode
Aries	Fire—courageous	Cardinal—pushy
Taurus	Earth—stable	Fixed—sedate
Gemini	Air—intellectual	Mutable—changeable
Cancer	Water—emotional	Cardinal—energetic
Leo	Fire—outgoing	Fixed—conforming
Virgo	Earth—process oriented	Mutable—adaptive
Libra	Air—sociable	Cardinal—active
Scorpio	Water—intuitive	Fixed—immovable
Sagittarius	Fire—enthusiastic	Mutable—flexible
Capricorn	Earth—constructive	Cardinal—action oriented
Aquarius	Air—idealistic	Fixed—stubborn
Pisces	Water—psychic	Mutable—chameleon-like

Again, repeat after me, "Hey, babe, what's your sign?" then furtively glance at this chart when she replies.

A final word on the sun sign: If you are a Cancer born on July 22 but feel more like a splashy Leo than a moist Crab, maybe you are indeed born under the sign of the proud Lion. What year were you born? You see, the sun changes signs every thirty to thirty-two days, shifting boundaries from one sign to another from year to year. This is why, if you were born "on the cusp" (two to three days before the end or the beginning of a sign), you may find that your sun sign varies from astrology book to astrology book, depending upon what year the book was written. Do yourself a favor if you are a cusp girl and either contact an astrologer or a local astrology school, or check an ephemeris book for your particular birth year. An ephemeris maps the movement of the planets through the signs on a daily basis for every year. It's the only way to know for sure what sign you really are.

To make your life easier, each sign chapter ends with a page describing the personality of those mysterious gals who are born on the cusp.

first step, sun sign. next step, the entire chart

The purpose of this book is to provide a full description of sun sign characteristics and personality traits—the good, the bad and the ugly. As you can see, locating your sun sign is relatively easy; just match it to your birthdate.

But that's not all there is to astrology, girlfriends. The truth is that there is quite a bit of astrological life beyond the sun sign; we have every planet and many different signs contained in our complete birth chart. To learn even more about yourself (or someone else) strike a deal with an astrologer and get a copy of your (or her) complete natal chart. You will need more than just a birthday however; you'll need a full birthdate (with the *exact* year), birth time, and birthplace. Since no one is born at the exact same time at the exact same place, a natal (or birth) chart is unique to each individual just like a set of fingerprints. Now we're cooking with oil! For those intrepid souls who care to take the next astrological step, please check out my website at www.AccessNewAge.com/Stargayzer for details on how to order a natal chart and full analysis.

The major components of a birth chart are *houses, planets, signs* and *aspects.* Houses represent where something is happening, planets show what is happening, signs show how it is happening and aspects show why it is happening. We've taken a swing at the signs for most of this introduction. Houses, planets and aspects are now in the batter's box.

The astrological chart looks like a pie divided into twelve slices. These slices are called *houses* and represent different areas of our life. All the planets are dispersed through this house system like guests or squatters.

House Areas of Influence

First	How you appear to others, first impressions and the beginning of things
Second	Money and finances; what you value
Third	How you communicate
Fourth	Your home, security and ancestors
Fifth	How you have fun, how you are creative and romantic
Sixth	Your job, health, pets and subordinates at work
Seventh	Partnerships and any one-to-one relationships
Eighth	Sex and deep psychological issues
Ninth	Travel, higher education, philosophical and legal issues
Tenth	Your career and long-term goals; status in the community
Eleventh	Friends and large social groups
Twelfth	Spirituality; personal secrets or hidden enemies

Lesbian astrology doesn't stop at the simple house classifications. In fact, my sapphic sisters, three of the above houses have what I refer to as *closets.* The fourth house, because it represents family and ancestors, contains the "family closet" that can suppress our pride because we are afraid of what Mom, Dad and the rest of the straight crew may think, say or do. The eighth house, because it harbors our sexuality, contains our "sexual closet" that can stifle our physical fulfillment and intimate connections with others. The twelfth house, because it represents hidden enemies and things we hide from ourselves, is perhaps our most personally destructive "psychological closet." It can keep us from emotional and spiritual affirmation by conjuring up demons of what-ifs, even when the what-ifs may in fact be why-the-heck-nots? Each sun sign chapter in this book has a full analysis of each sign's closeted issues under the heading, "Shhh—Secrets and Fears." Check them out and deal with them.

Here is a brief listing of the major planets and what energies they manifest as they meander through the many houses in your astrological chart.

planet areas of dominance

Sun	Personality; mission in life
Moon	How you express your emotions
Mercury	How you think and communicate
Venus	How you love and express love
Mars	How you fight or take action
Jupiter	Where you are lucky and where things are easy pickings
Saturn	Where you feel inadequate or have problems
Neptune	When you have foggy thinking or delusions
Uranus	Where you have surprises in your life
Pluto	Your power point of volcanic change and transformation

So, if you have a chatty, carefree Gemini sun but have dour Saturn in secretive Scorpio in the third house of communication, chances are you measure your words very carefully and may even have a fear of public speaking. Go figure!

Each of the following sun sign chapters in this book has a "Vital Statistics" section that lists, among other things, each sign's ruling planet, ruling house, element and mode. This is happily provided for those of us with lousy memories. "Vital Statistics" also includes lucky numbers, flowers, birthstones and even colors for each sign to help you in the birthday gift department. Also, just to pique your curiosity, I have included the tarot card most closely associated with that sign to give you further sign dimension.

Aspects are the electricity between the planets in your chart. Some planets are so close to one another that they rub, chafe, and ultimately cause sparks to fly. Others are positioned at just the right angles and happily coexist with their respective energies. Dust off your protractor, babe, and try your hand at measuring your aspects. I tend to restrict aspect analysis to the following major five angles: conjunction, sextile (one of my favs), square, trine and opposition. We can get into many, many others, including quincunx (Hey, who are you calling a cunx??!!), semisquares, semiconjuncts and a variety of other difficult ones but why bother? Life is stressful enough!

Aspect	Degrees Between Signs	Meaning
Conjunction	0	Difficult—minor collision, clash, pop!
Sextile	60	Easy—harmony, opportunities
Square	90	Difficult—barriers, stress
Trine	120	Easy—peaceful relationship
Opposition	180	Difficult—push me/pull you, at odds, stress

Flunked geometry? Don't worry, I'm not going to quiz you on aspects. Simply knowing that they exist may be helpful in case you decide to study astrology further.

Here's one more thing to keep you up at night: Common astrological wisdom states that the sun sign reflects our basic personalities, but in fact women tend to reflect the characteristics of the sign of their moon until they reach the age of thirty. For you sweet young things under the age of thirty, find out what sign your moon is in and read that sign chapter along with your sun sign chapter. The moon changes signs every couple of days so consult an ephemeris to locate your moon sign.

After the age of thirty (which marks the end of our Saturn Return—three years of excruciating change—which I explain and explore in the next section), we take on more of the characteristics of our sun sign. It's a glorious rebirth where we can feel our oats and maybe even the oats of a few bosom buddies as well. They say women over thirty blossom and have the ability and the wherewithal to attain their greatest dreams. When you are serious about settling down, choose a fully developed woman over thirty. There is no one better!

The Saturn Return

I would be derelict in my astrological duties if I did not mention the Saturn Return phase of our lives.

Saturn is the planet of discipline and impacts areas in our life where we feel inadequate or afraid. However, it also indicates where we learn hard-fought lessons as a result of difficult experiences. It is a rap on our knuckles, a stone in our lace-up hiking boots and a post-breakup Saturday night with a silicon toy with no batteries. Any place where Saturn resides in our birth chart is where we feel especially vulnerable, depressed or afraid. Nice, eh? The great thing about Saturn, if you can call it great, is that it is also considered the über teacher of the galaxy. Learn your lessons and you can graduate to the next step. Screw up, young lady, and you can stay after class and repeat (and repeat and repeat) the lesson. Ouch! Remember, you need to look at your complete natal chart to see in what house Saturn sits and what sign it is in.

There comes a point, every twenty-eight years or so (at ages twenty-eight, fifty-six and for the lucky few, eighty-four), when the planet Saturn, orbiting the sun in the cosmos, *makes a conjunct aspect* (did you pay attention to the paragraph on aspects?) to our natal Saturn. The effects of the Saturn Return last about two years like a slow-moving monster emerging from the muddy depths. So if you meet a frantic twenty-nine-year-old (or are a frantic twenty-nine-year-old yourself), go with the flow for another year no matter how painful it may feel. Things are shifting and changing so fast that you couldn't harness bedrock if you tried. (And, in retrospect, you may not want to park at that particular rocky bed.) Oh and another thing, relationships begun during a Saturn Return tend not to last. But they do provide interesting catty reappraisals and recriminations later. Lucky you.

Saturn helps us come to grips with our deepest fears, whether we want to or not. If we face these fears head on, we emerge from this period of life stronger and more enlightened. During a particular Saturn cycle, we will face unavoidable situations that will make us face our fears and provide essential life lessons. Don't ya just love those life lessons?

The Saturn Return heralds the end of a major life cycle and ushers in a period of great reevaluation, change and endings. You will have to ask yourself big and scary questions like: Are you living your life true to your own self or are you living in other people's "straight"-jackets? Use this time to review your life, whether it be in relationships, career, residence or family. But think rather than do. Don't begin anything new at this time (like a marriage or a new career) because there is just too much static on the line. Just use the time to reassess and ride the swelling tide.

In which house does Saturn sit in your natal chart? Once you obtain a copy of your birth chart, check the house chart in the prior section. That will give you a clue as to where most of this turmoil originates.

The good part is, as this cycle comes to a close you'll begin to reap what you have sown. You see, it has a happy ending, just like all those horror movies. Relax. Learn to expand your perspective and brace yourself for enforced changes, possible endings, and ongoing challenges and crises. Then make way for a time of new opportunities, new realizations, solidification and strengthening of foundations, new beginnings and maturity. Wisdom makes a great teacher, sister.

A final word

If you have any questions or comments about this book or about astrology in general, or have an interest in a personal reading or compatibility analysis, please contact me via e-mail at Lichtenstein@AccessNewAge.com. My website at www.AccessNewAge.com/Stargayzer has new horoscopes every month and you can also send a free on-line astrological greeting card to a particular cutie.

P.S. In case you were wondering, I'm Sagittarius, moon in Aquarius and Leo ascendant. Big mouth, big ideas, big ego. But let's not go there.

> pick battles big enough to matter,
> small enough to win.
> —Jonathan Kozol

✳

Aries

March 21–April 19
Rambunctious Dykes

Vital Statistics

Element = fire (energetic, action oriented)

Mode = cardinal (conceives of and creates change)

Ruling planet = Mars (the planet of action, aggression, pioneer spirit)

Ruling House = first (the house of beginnings, first impressions, physical appearance, childhood)

Ruling part of the Body = Head

Birthstone = Aquamarine (March) or diamond (April)

Best Day = Tuesday

Lucky Number = 1

Astral color = Red, white, rose, pink

Flower = Daffodil

Tarot card = Emperor IV (strong, driving, tenacious, the one in charge)

☾

🐏 The wise ancient seers dubbed those born between approximately March 21 and April 19 Aries the Ram, the first sign of the zodiac.

Ares to the Greeks (Mars to the Romans) was the god of war. The Greeks had a relatively low opinion of Ares, finding him to be a bloodthirsty, ruthless and cowardly kind of guy who lived by the motto He who pillages and runs away, lives to pillage another day. The Romans held him in higher esteem, referring to him as a great and invincible warrior who would never stoop so low as to beg for mercy in a lost battle. My personal opinion is that whatever his failings are, Ares is a pretty important deity. He was, after all, the father of the strong and courageous Amazons, those mythological Xenas who are permanent fixtures in my wet dreams. So even if his bird is the vulture, you have to cut him some slack. Hey, Dad, can I date your daughter?

general personality and first impressions

What all of this means is that amazon Aries are a mixture of spit and fire in a black leather G-string. They are the most determined and directed of all women (read: stubborn) and are loath to give up even when the battle seems hopelessly lost. Without a doubt, they are the women I want on my side in any fight. Of course, they are also the pushiest, most domineering and bossiest gals on the planet. Generally they are about as subtle as a panzer tank or a pickax.

And why shouldn't they be aggressive? After all they are numero uno—the first sign of the zodiac, ruler of the head and symbolized by the Ram who butts first and asks questions later. One of the most refreshing things about this gal is that what you see is what you get; no sneaky Scorp, she. What it also means is that she is pretty much an open book. For those of you who prefer flirtatious mind games, forgetaboutit with this lass and find yourself a

Gemini or Pisces. Who the heck has time for such nonsense? Let's get down to business . . . or let's just get down!

You can always spot a sapphic Ram by her strong, bold, proud and forthright appearance. There she stands with shoulders squared, her hands on her ample hips, practically begging for a confrontation. But the truth is, sister, that these gals are usually as ready for a bear hug or something a bit warmer and wetter. They have an immense capacity for love and affection and a robust sexual appetite, if you decide to give them a taste. Don't let their aggressively feisty appearance dissuade you; they are lambs between the sheets . . . and on the kitchen table . . . and on the beach . . . and even on a small glass coffee table. Say a few sweet words in her ear and you could be feasting on broiled lamb chops every night of the week.

She is rather particular when it comes to her wardrobe and will dress for any occasion. For this reason it is hard to categorize her; she can run the gamut, from overalls and Birkenstocks to a hot little strapless number. Anything to make a point and command a presence. She is not big on bangles and bows but will have a few pieces of chunky jewelry that highlight her coloring or have some sentimental value. Whatever she decides to wear, she will fill it out nicely; Ram sisters are full-bodied mamas. Swirl her goblets and take a sip.

Her politics can span the political spectrum but don't be surprised if she's generally more conservative than most when it comes to issues such as gun control (not!). This militaristic mama needs access to her fire power and she secretly carries pictures of Charlton Heston in her wallet. As she gets older she gets more stubborn and entrenched, so ply her politics while she's young and emotionally supple if you want to try to change her position.

career and work

Because Aries is the ruler of the first house of new beginnings and first impressions, sapphic Rams are happiest in careers where they can be fire starters, getting projects off the ground with a rousing, passionate boost. With all this independent energy, it is understandable that these amazon Rams are not particularly good at taking orders and will give a fiery mouth to any imbecile who tries to order them around. For that reason, expect your Arian woman to be self-employed or working in a situation where she doesn't have a direct boss. For those unfortunate types who for one reason or another have to labor in the bowels of the mailroom or some other powerless position, their job will be the least important aspect of their life and they will treat it as such.

In past lives this gal might have been a swashbuckler, pirate or explorer. Now you may find her in the police or fire department, in the armed forces or in other jobs where she can manifest her own destiny. Gore is no prob for this sister: She is the butchest butcher in town and, because Aries rules the head, she can also be found among brain surgeons. Sapphic Rams are also rather adept at mechanics. Ask one to tune your engine and you won't be disappointed.

Aries gals are prime candidates to be small-business owners or entrepreneurs where they can build something wonderful from the ground up. But they are not necessarily the most creative types and would do well to work in a partnership where the combination of thought and action can be used to greatest effect. Aries women tend to be all action and less thought than one would hope. Pairing up with an air sign (Gemini, Aquarius or Libra) may help catapult the business to new heights. Like most fire signs, Rambo mamas also often lack follow-through, charging ahead full force only to lose interest halfway down the road. For that reason, a business partnership with a slow and steady earth sign (Taurus, Capricorn or Virgo) may, in certain circumstances, give this girl more sustained professional oomph.

Barring owning their own business or working for the government, sapphic Rambos should consider a career in sales where performance is based on delivery rather than on political acumen or sucking up. Like all other fire signs (Leo and Sagittarius) Aries gals are too honest, forthright and proud to be smarmy and obsequious to authority. We leave that to the Capricorns. Bette Davis and Joan Crawford were both Aries and they did it their way, beautifully.

money

One thing that these women learned early in life is that money is power, and the more of it the better. They are not above buying and selling people or things to get their way, but they are so darn obvious about it that you can't be too insulted or get very angry with them. Some might even say, go with the flow and enjoy the fun.

Aries dykes can behave like kids in a candy store but are fairly generous, if they think that you support them unconditionally. For this reason it is very easy to take advantage of them. Sadly, it takes a rather long time for these trusting souls to catch on to a scam because they tend to be blind to manipulation. However, once they figure out that they've been used and abused, they will take no prisoners and will never ever forget. Woe betide the person who takes advantage of our willful Ram sister.

If they can keep tabs on their swag, these women have the ability to parlay their hard work into an easy early retirement. But even in retirement, they will never be lethargic; you'll see them working at least part time or as a consultant for the rest of their lives. Why? Because they like it!

Aries is a cardinal sign which means that they create and enforce change. What better way to move folks than to ply them with money. What better way to grease the wheels of change than with a dollop of cash? Amazon Aries love to use their money to move great causes forward whether it's for breast cancer research, AIDS awareness, domestic abuse prevention or abortion rights. But let's not discuss those secret donations to the NRA . . .

The Aries Home

The typical Aries home has large pieces of functional furniture, nicely arranged so she can usually be at the command center. Her entertainment center is state of the art and, needless to say, the bigger the better: Why have a fifteen-inch television when a fifteen-footer will do? (All the better to watch wrestling . . . or Xena.) Don't be surprised (or put off) to find that her favorite piece of furniture is a large, naugahyde La-Z-Boy recliner, which holds a prominent place in her living or family room. Eventually, you may be able to relegate it to the basement, along with her bowling trophy collection and wagon-wheel coffee table.

For this reason, expect to find her in the suburbs, a small town or the country, where she can have a rec room basement, two- or three-car garage for all her assorted vehicles (car, motorcycle, snowmobile and some old wreck that she's been working on for years) and a state-of-the-art workshop with all the latest power tools and gadgets. I hope she doesn't live in New York City where even those of us who are out of the closet have to rent one as an apartment. This woman needs room to roam.

An Aries woman doesn't mind cooking and can become a fairly accomplished chef if given the opportunity. Chefs are, after all, the big bosses in the kitchen . . . hmmmm. She is a superb entertainer and often plans large dinner parties and get-togethers with her bosom buddies. *Nouvelle,* she is not. Expect meat, meat and more meat. You want a salad? Have a pickle!

Love, sex and Relationships

When a Rambo girl loves you, she loves you with all her heart and soul. There is no coy approach, no funny games or any cat and mouse pas de deux unless she's doing the deuxing. She probably will have a mere handful of lovers throughout her life (unlike fickle Gemini who can count them into the thousands) and can remain loyal as long as she doesn't feel taken advantage of. Flirtation, if it comes at all, will manifest itself in the early stages of a relationship. As soon as she is comfortable, she gets down to basics and business.

Modesty is not a strong suit with this gal, so don't be surprised if she hangs around the house in her all-togethers . . . or less. But expect her usual form to be boxer shorts rather than a peekaboo lace teddy. The fire of passion will always be there, but it may be camouflaged in flannel. Hey, honey, pass the beer! Yeah, I love you too. Burp! But make her jealous, nervous or unsure and she'll dress in peel-away zippered black leather, just to make sure that you notice and still care. What a charmer!

Young or less-experienced lesbian Rams need to learn how to go the distance in a relationship. They generally lack a long-term attention span and are more sporadic brush fire than eternal flame. (Oh but they can set underbrush on fire, sister!) Sometimes the pursuit is more gratifying than the conquest. (Well, actually more gratifying than the morning after the conquest when both of you need to brush your teeth . . .) But once you hook this girl in her craw, which is not utterly impossible, she is yours forever. She is the most loyal of the fire signs.

Rub her head and tell her how powerful, masterful and courageous she is. Rub her fountainhead and tell her how sexy, strong and delicious she is. Then pretend that you are a territory ready to be conquered and let her bombs explode in your trenches. Take no prisoners, lovergrrl.

friends

There is no more inspirational friend than an Aries dyke. She will always be there to give a bosom buddy a strong shoulder for support and an affirming word of encouragement. Hers is an open, unfettered friendship based on mutual respect, honesty and loyalty. Need to move a houseful of furniture? Car won't start? Getting over a painful breakup? Call an Aries. She'll apply the muscle where necessary and get your mind off emotional mind games with strenuously fun outdoor activities.

She is the captain of the team, the coach and the manager. If women were allowed to play professional football, she'd be the first female quarterback (and do better than some of the specimens we have now). Expect to see her barking orders to her teammates at her weekend softball game. Come to think of it, her team always wins.

Lesbian Rams like to surround themselves with galpals who are followers and supporters. She ascribes to the old saying "Too many cooks spoil the broth" or, in this case, "Too many generals. No tanks!" She likes to command the group dynamic and tends to infuse it with energy and direction. All for one and one for all, and I'm in charge, honey!

Her loyalty enables her to maintain good, solid friendships over the years. Don't be surprised if she introduces you to some latently homophobic suburban matron she's known since kindergarten (I suppose that there's no accounting for tastes).

family and parents

Rambo dykes may have experienced difficulties in their childhood if their parents tried to rein them in or quash their innate enthusiasm or sense of leadership. They are one of the few signs who rebel against parental authority and they do not take kindly to boundaries, curfews and rules (unless of course they make them . . . or think they make them).

Smart parents gave these girls plenty of room to maneuver and built up their confidence so they strove for accomplishment rather than destruction. Sensible parental advice: Accept these magnificent girls for who they are and allow them to make their own decisions within reason; they will grow up to be confident and happy adults.

As young things, their rooms were probably decorated in early military. Planes, ships, tanks and other assorted hardware competed for shelf space with dirty socks, elbow and knee pads, smelly jerseys and assorted sports equipment. Neat, they weren't . . . and aren't. Don't expect this Jane to take up the piano, violin or harp. Give her a trumpet or a set of drums and she's in heaven.

In school, these girls were youthful mavericks, excelling in sports, history and mechanics and leaving English, penmanship and art to Libra and Taurus. They might have tried a run for student government or captain of the girl's basketball team. And no field hockey team would be complete without a brazen and bold sapphic Ram wielding a stick.

communication style

As with other fire signs, Rambo sisters are loud, proud and queer when it comes to communications. They say what's on their mind, come what may, and are not averse to backing up their opinion with a few physical exclamation points to accentuate their positions on love or on war. Honesty and integrity are par for the course.

Sapphic Rams speak with authority and don't mince words. They command rather than ask, which can drive some women crazy, especially Virgos. (Ever hear of the words *please* and *thank you?)* They don't mean to be impolite; they are just focused on getting the point across and the faster the better.

Subtle nuance is not in their repertoire. Charm, style and panache are fine for Libras or Gemini, but a true amazon Aries is short on acrobatic finesse. Why tickle with a feather when tossing an anvil would do just fine; and it's faster! She is the one best suited to lead a pride march. I suspect it was an Aries who tossed the first brick at Stonewall in 1969. Hey, it made the point!

Health and Fitness

Not surprisingly, these gals have rather robust constitutions, but they often don't know when to stop and rest. Even if they feel like they are on their last leg, they can still be persuaded to surge forward for one last reckless battle or altruistic rescue. They also have a tendency to take on too many enemies at once, biting off more than they can easily chew (tempting as it may be). Take it easy? What planet are you living on, babe?

Sapphic Rams expend great energy in short bursts. They can do the hundred-yard dash but are not well-suited to a marathon. Scorpio gals, for instance, attack by coming and retreating, coming and retreating, coming and retreating, until the ocean eats away the shore. (Whew, I need a cigarette.) An Aries woman prefers to lob a few grenades, storm the beaches, upend the landscape, kill a few luckless enemies and then crash in exhaustion.

For this reason, they are more prone to accidents than most other signs. They court danger, and sometimes danger bites back. They are also prone to headaches, eye strain, sinus attacks, mental stress and, at worst, panic attacks brought on by excessive fatigue. Sometimes they are just prone, which happens to be the way I prefer to see them . . .

However, as much as these gals may be hurting, they are no

long-suffering Camilles quietly wheezing and daintily coughing up sputum in their lace hankies. They are loud and demanding patients with full bedpans. Piss and moan. I want. I want. I want. Hey, my head is killing me. Where's my body massage? Brace yourself during flu season if your galpal is an ailing Aries.

shhh—secrets and fears

Let's peek into the astrological closets of an amazon Aries. The areas of her solar chart that contain feelings of guilt, repression, ancestral baggage or family pressure are ruled by sensitive water signs. This means that, despite all outward appearances of robust strength, the Aries woman needs a tremendous amount of sensitivity and tender loving care for her to attain her fully affirmed potential. Sexually, she is a passionate, sensual and jealous tigress, but she would rather pull out her toenails than admit to possessiveness. Spiritually, she yearns for religion or some other standardized framework where she is made to feel at one with the cosmos. Soft and mushy? Iron-fisted amazon Aries? Shhh.

When it comes to family, she is mother to all and responds on a visceral level to the parent who nurtured and smothered her. At heart, she poses as an independent force but deep down longs to be tamed, protected or owned. She will never admit this, even under threat of torture (like taking away her *Monday Night Football*).

Aries are also deathly afraid of publicly displayed personal failure. (Chances are you will never see her on *Jerry Springer*. We leave that to approval-seeking Libras.) There is nothing so embarrassing to otherwise proud Rams than to have their dirty laundry aired out for all to see, or to have a disastrous professional setback in front of an audience. This is a sign of weakness and must be avoided at all costs.

At heart, they strive for acceptance from the powers that be. They may not be as recklessly individualistic as they make themselves out to be. In fact, in some sorry, self-pitying instances, they can be quite conformist.

For this sad reason, some afflicted Aries sisters may have a difficult time coming out. Their fear of failure and rejection sometimes overtakes their better judgment and long-term peace of mind. A good friend or faithful lover will help this proud woman attain her fullest, affirmed potential. Then, once she's pumped up with confidence, step back and let her conquer the world.

weaknesses: are there any?

At their worst, Aries dykes can be petty tyrants, drama queens and schoolyard bullies who think nothing of picking an easy fight with a weaker, injured opponent or bespectacled neighborhood geek. Some astrology books say that Adolf Hitler was an Aries. (He was, in fact, a Taurus right on the cusp of Aries, so go figure.)

Like other fire signs, Aries women are not particularly good at keeping secrets and display impatience with those who dream about things instead of doing them. They can be spoilsports, stepping on sand castles and peeing on sidewalk chalk designs. Really extreme types can become neighborhood cranks whose idea of civic outreach is to sandblast a rusted relic in their front yard so the neighbors can watch . . . *and learn a thing or two.*

and in conclusion

For pure spit and fire, look no further than an amazon Aries. This spirited gal will take you to places that you might have dreamed of but never thought you could attain. What she lacks in long-term romance she will heartily make up for in loyalty and ongoing lust (if you know how to stoke that engine). Let her stake her claim on your life. Without her, life would go nowhere and be *boring*.

Lucy Lawless - March 29

stand aside, ladies: xena the warrior princess is here to save the day. can there be a better example of a strong willed powerhouse of an Aries woman than Lawless, who plays xena on television? i can picture her, muscles rippling under her tight, barely-there outfit, and itching for a fight. This gal knows what she is looking for and is not afraid of pursuing her dreams and righting wrongs. Lawless herself is a pretty tough and resilient mama. growing up in a household full of brothers forced her to hold her own in rough and tumble play. pioneering and confident, she's the quintessential Aries poster girl. But even as you gaze at all that loveliness, remember that Lawless is married . . . to a man. sob!

Relationships with other signs

While it is necessary to examine the entire horoscope in any relationship, it *is* possible to make some crass generalizations about sun sign compatibilities. Read ahead, girlfriend, but take it all with a grain of salt.

Aries and Aries—When two Aries dykes get together it can either be a match made in heaven or a match to light a bomb. Who will relinquish the TV remote? Who will make all the decisions? In business, this combination is unbeatable, although details like who pays the bills should be delegated to a Virgo accountant. Sexual sparks fly in love. Thank goodness sapphic Rams are less concerned about being loved for their intellect.

Aries and Taurus—Lesbian Bulls may be too slow-moving and thoughtful for the fiery, impetuous lambda Ram. A successful business partnership is possible because one will be happy to plod along at the pedantic tasks while the other goes out and imperialistically conquers new territory. In love, romantic Taurean gals may have their roses crushed and champagne spilled by a Ram stampede to the bedroom. Some of us like a quick muff buff, some of us don't.

Aries and Gemini—An Aries-Gemini combination is said to be a good match in both love and business. Both are independent and energetic but in different, complementary ways: Lambda Rams are more physical, sapphic Twins are more intellectual. Love relationships can be passionate but the heat can subside quickly. Suggestion: Stock up on crotchless panties and extra-wide beef jerky.

Aries and Cancer—Unthinking, independent Aries dykes can ride roughshod over the delicate emotional makeup of a sapphic Cancer lass. There may be frayed nerves in a business relationship as the reckless, feckless Aries creates tension and worry for conservative Cancer. In love, the Cancer mama is willing to serve and aching to nurture. The Aries Amazon is willing to be served but can't be reined in. How long can it go on?

Aries and Leo—These two fiery ladies make an unbeatable pair in both business and love. There is a tacit understanding that each one needs her personal space and individual victories, but there is also a mutual admiration society in which they cheer each other on and find ways of, *ahem,* vigorously celebrating together. Did someone mention zesty sex? Yes, please!

Aries and Virgo—Aries sisters like to create change while Virgo dykes accept it and go with the flow. In business, sapphic Rams tend to upset the applecart while lesbian Virgins try to make do with applesauce. How long will our long-suffering Virgo put up with such cheap abuse? The same situation is true in love: Aries women are out for energetic adventure while lambda Virgos are content with a hot toddy and a vibrator. Whose battery will run out first?

Aries and Libra—The Aries-Libra combination works well in both business and in love. In business, the domineering, pioneering Aries mama is carefully steered in the right direction by the suave hand of a level-headed lesbian Libra. In love, flirtatious gay Libras can keep a lusty sapphic Ram right where they want her: in line, in bed or in limbo waiting for the next hint. Hint, hint.

Aries and Scorpio—For the independent Aries dyke, the manipulative manner of a sapphic Scorpio may come as a rude awakening. In business, these two will never quite trust each other: Scorpio babes will be convinced that their Aries partner is giving away the store while Aries dykes will be sure that their Scorpio sister is underhanded and entirely too secretive. You can only guess how a love relationship would progress!

Aries and Sagittarius—The feisty combination of these two independent and honest souls works well in both business and in love. In both situations, they work as equal partners, understanding and forgiving foibles and, in the case of Sagittarius, general uncouthness. The sex is robust and more physically passionate than emotionally romantic. Hey, champagne only gives the proud Archer gas anyway.

Aries and Capricorn—Aries dykes have a tendency to stress out conservative lesbian Caps. In business arrangements, the proud Ram is always willing to take risks while worrywart Goats sweep up the shattered glass. In love, the Ram has a tendency to run roughshod over sensitive sapphic Goats. Neither are great on long-term compromise, so let's agree to disagree. Get out of my way, sister!

Aries and Aquarius—When these two wellsprings get together there is a real meeting of the minds. One has the grand visionary scheme and the other has the energy and stamina to make it happen. In business, the lambda Ram has a comrade in arms in the sapphic Aquarian. Same thing in love, except it's called a babe in arms.

Aries and Pisces—Aries dykes have a tendency to unintentionally quash the dreams and hopes of Pisces gals. Maybe it's because one is so practical and the other is so, well, impractical. This arrangement works better in love than in business because love always seems to conquer all. It all depends on how long the Pisces woman can delude herself that this is right for her.

famous Aries: one a Day

Rosie O'Donnell	talk-show host, actor	March 21
Stephen Sondheim	songwriter	March 22
Joan Crawford	actor	March 23
Grethe Cammermeyer	nurse, soldier	March 24
Gloria Steinem	feminist	March 25
Sandra Day O'Connor	Supreme Court Justice	March 26
Mariah Carey	singer	March 27
Dirk Bogarde	actor	March 28
Lucy Lawless	actor	March 29
Warren Beatty	actor	March 30
Barney Frank	politician, congressman	March 31
Ali MacGraw	actor	April 1
Camille Paglia	writer	April 2
Doris Day	actor, singer	April 3
Kitty Kelly	writer	April 4
Bette Davis	actor	April 5
Harry Houdini	illusionist	April 6
Janis Ian	singer	April 7
Betty Ford	first lady	April 8
Hugh Hefner	entrepreneur	April 9
Clare Boothe Luce	politician, ambassador	April 10
Louise Lasser	actor	April 11
David Letterman	talk-show host	April 12
Thomas Jefferson	president	April 13
Loretta Lynn	singer	April 14
Leonardo da Vinci	artist	April 15
Ellen Barkin	actor	April 16
Cynthia Ozick	poet	April 17
Mildred Bailey	brigadier general	April 18
Jayne Mansfield	actor	April 19

women born on the cusp

Those born between April 16 and April 22 tend to have a combination of Aries and Taurus attributes.

The mixture of the hot energy of Aries and the persevering determination of Taurus gives these sapphic women unparalleled courage, hardheadedness and an overwhelming sense of purpose in life. These gals wouldn't know the meaning of the words *no, nyet, nein* or even *non,* even if you tried to explain them. Some may say that she is pushy, but let's chalk it up to a fierce determination to win at all costs. The Aries Bull has one of the strongest personalities of any lass in the zodiac, possessing a sharp mind to boot. She always knows best and thinks nothing of graciously offering her pearls of wisdom to any oyster in need of a protective shell.

She carries this determination into all areas of her life and has what is arguably the strongest sex drive of any planetary combination. So thank your lucky stars when she trots in your direction; her stamina is unmatched. She is also one of the great cosmic healers if you allow her fingers to do the, *ahem,* probing.

The miracle is not to fly in the air or to walk on the water but to walk on the earth.
—chinese proverb

TauruS

April 20—May 20

The Sensuous Bull

Vital Statistics

Element = Earth (stable, functional, process oriented)

Mode = Fixed (fights change, attempts stability)

Ruling planet = Venus (the planet of beauty, love and art)

Ruling House = Two (the house of money and our value system)

Ruling part of the Body = Mouth, throat and neck

Birthstone = Diamond (April) or emerald (May)

Best Day = Friday

Lucky Number = 2

Astral color = Brown, red, lemon yellow

Flower = sweet pea

Tarot card = The Hierophant V (clear thinker, very stubborn, successful)

The wise ancient seers dubbed those born between approximately April 20 and May 20 Taurus the Bull, the second sign of the zodiac.

When I think of Taurus I think of the story of Europa who was literally carried away by a sexually aroused Zeus disguised as a beautiful and sweet-smelling bull. Europa was astonishingly voluptuous and Zeus was in the business of collecting voluptuous women. It is difficult to say how Europa could be so naive as to climb on the back of an attractive but strange bull based on the persistently probing nudges of its snout, but I suppose we all fall prey to that sort of temptation at one time or another. Zeus carried her to Crete where he essentially set her up as his mistress and concubine. Some bulls have all the luck!

general personality and first impressions

What this means is that Taurus the Bull is an earthy woman guided by insatiable appetites that strive to be amply fulfilled whether it's for love, companionship, lust, food, drink or just plain day-to-day living. She is generous, genial, gorgeous and blessed with exquisite taste and style. Of course, there are those afflicted types that buck the Taurean trend and spend their days dining on frozen fishsticks, canned ravioli and Thunderbird, but they just may be waiting for the right dinner invitation. Generally, these gals know how to live well and aspire to have enough money to support their lavish lifestyles and a randy girlfriend and still have a bit in the bank for a rainy day.

Sapphic Bulls are very comfortable with their bodies and dress for success. They wear anything well, even a burlap sack, but tend to favor warm-colored garments that flatter and accentuate their strong points. These gals tend to have round faces and bull-like behaviors or features. Don't laugh; their nostrils flare when they get angry. They have also been known to lounge around the house looking like a lazy Ferdinand smelling the flowers. However, as likable as Ferdinand is, these gals are by far my most favorite bulls.

She is not a firestarter. (That falls into Aries territory.) As a sedate earth sign, a Taurean dyke is more willing to take orders than to give them. But once you get her moving and on track, she displays a bulldog determination that guarantees success . . . eventually. Old-time astrologers call her stubborn, stubborn, stubborn, but I like to say she is persevering and relentless. Even in the face of insurmountable odds, she plods on . . . and on . . . and on, like an inexhaustible locomotive, until she attains her goal. The problem is that she is not particularly good at letting go and can waste considerable time and energy pursuing lost causes. (No names, please!) Of course tunnel vision has its advantages, especially if it's your tunnel she's envisioning. . . .

career and work

Because Taurus is the ruler of the second house of art, finances, objects of value and one's intrinsic value system, Taurean Bulls tend to gravitate to careers in which they can surround themselves with either warm, expensive objects or cold, hard cash. They have a good head for figures and a good eye for art, but they are not necessarily creative. For this reason, they can do well as antique dealers, art gallery owners, or auction house directors. Because these women are so trustworthy, they are often tapped as financial advisers and make excellent bankers, brokers, accountants or financial guardians.

Because Taurus is ruled by charismatic Venus and, in turn, rules the throat, one can find more than a few of these babes in the acting and singing professions. Michelle Pfeiffer, Cher and Barbra Streisand are all Tauruses, in case you were curious.

Unlike pushy Aries, Taurean mamas actually enjoy taking orders. This works out particularly well in sexual foreplay . . . and can also take her far up the corporate food chain. Like their opposite sign, Scorpio, lesbian Tauruses are good backroom political strategists and are often the powers behind the throne. Unlike maniacal Scorps, however, these bullish gals vie more for preferential treatment and perks than for raw power and control. Their ultimate goal is luxury, not stressful intrigue. Yet, there always seem to be a few divas in the herd. These gals more than likely have a few planets in Aries in their natal horoscopes.

These lovely ladies tend to underrate their considerable abilities and may need an initial push to get their careers jumpstarted. They are modest, hard-working and patient, and, happily, their true abilities eventually become evident and they reap some recognition for their efforts well before retirement. They are survivors by sheer instinct and dogged application.

money

An amazon Bull is perhaps the best money manager of the zodiac. If you have funds to invest, consult this sapphic woman. She will not put your life savings in derivatives or other high-risk money schemes. More than likely, she will carefully place your nest egg in a conservative money market or annuity. It may not triple in a year, but you are practically guaranteed to feast on fluffy omelets in your old age.

Sapphic Bulls are acquisitive sisters, avidly storing up their acorns for the inevitable winter. But, unlike careful Virgos, they tend to be fairly generous with their stash and can lavish all sorts of goodies on their girlfriends. They are not overly ostentatious or showy and don't flaunt their wealth. While Leo sisters get wet for the big splash, Taurean mamas seek comfort, utility and personal beauty . . . and that goes for both their material and amorous acquisitions.

Afflicted Bulls can, in fact, take this love of money and ease to a perverted next step. They can become very greedy and selfish, unable to share with others or enjoy their wealth on their own. These troubled souls can be found wearing old worn clothes, eating out of garbage cans (only in the best neighborhoods, mind you) and living on the streets as cheaply as possible with a hefty balance in their bank accounts.

The Taurean Home

Amazon Bulls need room to roam. For this reason, expect to find their spreads where they can spread out. Ranches, estates, or palatial homes in the suburbs will do just fine. Even in claustrophobic New York City, these gals manage to find larger-than-average apartments where they can stretch their legs and display their dust-collecting tchotchkes. Maybe that's why Park Slope, Brooklyn, with its large brownstone apartments, is such a popular neighborhood with these gals.

Their homes are a reflection of their wonderful and expensive tastes, their innate sense of design and form and their desire for comfort. Expect to see overstuffed easy chairs, rich carpeting, stylish decoration and objets d'art. There will be many "earth-related" items around (given that they are the earthiest of earth signs), such as pottery, plants and landscapes. It will always be clean and neat with everything in its place. Unlike sloppy Sags, these sisters need order and serenity surrounding them at home. Don't even think of leaving your dirty socks on your pillow!

Plant your Taurus on the couch and a couch potato will sprout. Lead her to the kitchen and you will be seduced by some of the best cooking this side of the continent. While she is not especially experimental or creative (forget food with edible flowers or funny colors), she is excellent at following recipes and knows all the wonderful little details that make her dinner parties sought-after invitations. She loves to entertain and does so often. For this reason, her home not only has a large, well-appointed kitchen but also a large dining room.

She is rather handy around the house, plastering walls, repairing cabinetry and greasing locks. While Libra sisters mix the drinks and plan the color scheme, Taurean mamas rewire the house and install the second bathroom. But most of the time you can find these fireplugs parked in front of the tube contemplating the ballgame scores.

love, sex and relationships

Hubba hubba. Lesbian Bulls are arguably some of the sexiest gals in the zodiac. Their ruling planet, Venus—the planet of love, beauty and art—gives them unfair advantage in the look and feel department. When they are inspired, they know how to dress for sexcess and seem to know just what buttons to push to get a gal overflowing with lust. Rub her tummy and kiss her face (especially on either side of her nose and under her eyes) and she'll follow you anywhere. She is inexhaustible and, like that pink bunny, can keep going and going and going. Hop on, hop off. Hop on, hop off. Whew!

These gals can be tempted to mud wrestle for their meal. They also quite enjoy watching other scantily clad babes take their turns in the mud pit. They will gladly help scrub-a-dub the winner, or even the loser. It's amazing where mud can hide!

After the ball is over, she can plotz in front of the tube with the best of them. Without stimulation, she can fall into a pattern of familiar malaise. Blow in her ear and she'll leave that warm cushion. Leave her to her own devices and she'll plow through a six-pack, a pizza and a tub of popcorn. The wise lover will give this gal lots of love, affection and attention. She may not be the most experimental lover but she has luxurious stamina and a romantic streak. Who else would try to fill your bathtub with champagne and fresh cherries as a Valentine surprise? (Certainly not Virgo—too messy!)

And a Taurean gal is loyal. Unlike those flirty air signs (Gemini, Libra or "Aqueerius"), Taurus is a one-woman woman. Quality, not quantity, is this gal's credo. However, she can be enticed by a cheap but attractive package if she's not getting her first-class delivery at home. Don't take advantage of or underestimate this modest babe. Remember, while it takes a while for her to latch on to something, once she sets her mind on a particular goal, it's difficult to pull her off.

Taurus is not the most expressive of women, so don't expect her to whisper naughty little nothings in your ear during love-making. We leave that to flirtatious Gemini. But what she lacks in style and cheap theatrics, she makes up for in a wellspring of emotional depth, honesty, devotion and a desire for permanence and monogamy. Supposedly still water runs deep and rapids are shallow. That about sums it up for the Taurean lovergrrl.

friends

Taurean gals tend to make long-lasting and loyal friendships. While she is not overly sentimental, don't be surprised if she carts out some ex-lovergrrl from aeons ago. This difficulty with cutting off from the past can be cured with better treatment in the present and more excitement in the future.

She has a conservative, clubby crew to pal around with. It's very likely that they travel as a group from large dinner parties to golf outings to the movies. All for one, one for all. You for me, me for you. Whatever! If she likes someone, it will not matter how obnoxious or odious they are; they are included in the revelry. She may have friends who have few other friends. On the flip side, if she gets pissed off with someone (or feels that she's being taken advantage of), the ties are broken. As steadfastly close as she can be to certain galpals she can be as steadfastly distant from enemies or those she dislikes.

family and parents
Unless she had a particularly unhappy childhood, this bullish gal tends to be very close to Mom and Pop and may follow their lead in many of life's directions. If she experienced a sedate homelife, having dinner at 6 P.M. every night, that's what she'll expect to have as an adult. Dad votes Republican? Hey, count me in! Mom favors mambo? Hot cha-cha! Happily, once she strays from home and transplants herself into her rightful neighborhood, it is possible to wean her off of some of the more ridiculous family credos. Lesbian Bulls are not good self-starters but they are good finishers and can learn to follow your lead.

Smart parents challenge these young girls by giving them projects and goals that may be slightly difficult but are not impossible to attain. They need that carrot on a stick when they are young and impressionable to help them build their confidence and stamina for adult success. When they're adults, they'll go for the challenge.

This fixation on family may be one reason why she may take longer than other signs to come out to parents and other relations. Fear of rejection runs rampant in this girl's psyche and she would have to feel very sure of acceptance before she took the leap. However, this does not mean she will stay closeted for life. Far from it. She will simply go her own way, lead her own life in these matters and leave it unspoken. It's not the perfect solution, but it's better than living in a childhood "straight"-jacket.

communication style

Taurean girlfriends are slow, steady and deliberate in their communication. Blessed by charismatic Venus (her ruling planet), this smooth operator can pose as a friend to all and charm even the surliest of beasts. Because she is so politically astute, she is generally very careful of her wording and tone of voice. For this reason, she makes an excellent public relations front. You may never know when she absolutely hates someone. That's her little secret!

Generally speaking, sapphic Tauruses are not interested in arguing simply for the sake of blowing wind. We leave that to the windy air signs (Aquarians, Libras or Gemini) who enjoy hearing themselves speak . . . and speak . . . and speak. Taurean babes think it is an unpleasant waste of time. They prefer to go for the goal; to argue only to win folks over to their side of an argument. They tend to succeed by sheer stamina and stubborness. Like other earth signs, sapphic Tauruses convince by pushing and pushing and pushing or, in the case when someone is trying to convince her, by remaining rock firm and immobile. Try taking her on sometime. Hey, knock yourself out!

This sister can usually keep a secret. For this reason, you have little to fear when confiding in her. Unlike some of the big-mouth signs (like Sagittarius) this mama is discreet and often insightful and helpful. She would never criticize or interfere but would simply be the repository of information, responding only when asked for her advice. She also judges no one, no matter how obscene one's policies may be. This can drive other, more judgmental signs (like Virgo and Aquarius) wild, but our placid Bull puts it all in perspective. It's no wonder that Sigmund Freud was a Taurus.

Health and fitness

With all that great cooking and a sedate lifestyle, Taurean dykes have a tendency to pile on the pounds as they get older. (There will just be more of them to love . . .) Get her off her duff every so often and have her walk around the block. (Ever try to push a bull around?) At the very least let her do most of the housework or most of the foreplay to build up a little sweat.

As you might have guessed, don't expect to see too many of these bullish gals huffing and puffing at the gym. You may find them stewing in the hot tub, schvitzing in the steam room, or "kneading" a massage, instead. Their tastes run more toward golf than tennis. At least in golf you get to ride around in a cart and have someone else lug your clubs around. When they get run down, which is not very often, they tend to overdramatize. Give her a hot toddy and a dose of sympathy and she'll be content to sprawl on the bed and snore the day away.

Some astrology books say that Tauruses are meat-and-potato mamas with large sweet tooths and generally poor diets, but I beg to differ. Their diet tends to reflect what Mother prepared for them as kids. If they ate steamed fish and salad as girls, they'll eat steamed fish and salad as women. If they ate a pound of steak, potatoes fried in lard and no vegetable to speak of . . . you get the idea.

shhh—secrets and fears

Here is a nasty little secret about lambda Bulls: The areas of their solar chart that contain feelings of guilt, repression, ancestral baggage or family pressure are ruled by feisty, reckless fire signs. This means that, despite all outward appearances of conformity and placidity, the Taurean woman secretly aches to break free of convention, pierce her nipples, dye her hair purple, prance around nude at work and charge at windmills. The astute lover will recognize that she secretly needs a tremendous amount of spark, spit and fire for her to attain her fully affirmed potential. Sexually she is a possessive and attentive lover but she would rather peel paint off with her tongue than admit that zippered masks and tight, black leather crotchless panties turn her on. Jump-start her secret desires and she will be revving your engine forever!

When she loses control of a situation, emotional outbursts erupt like a blazing fire, leaving a trail of charred and ashen remains. Some signs, like Sagittarius, get off on that sort of thing, but conservative Bulls feel chewed up when they are thrown off track like that.

weaknesses: are There any?

Aside from being stubborn, stubborn, stubborn, Taurean dykes can be very reactionary and conservative, especially as they grow older. Fear of risk, fear of change, fear of instability (read: excitement) can immobilize them and deep-freeze their progress. And try to pry one of these babes off her carefully bricked-up position once she's made up her mind! Forgetaboutit, sister; it would be easier to plow through the Himalayas.

A pleasant evening with one of these immobilized Bulls may consist of television, television and more television. Why play golf when you can watch in the comfort of you own home? Leave her to her own devices and she will plan her day around inactivity: resting, napping, snoozing and maybe a nosh or two or three or ten. No, that's not an undulating throw rug drinking a beer; that's a Taurean babe doing stomach curling exercises . . . while drinking a beer.

She can be rather, *ahem,* earthy, which is a polite way of saying crude. Don't expect a debonair Ginger Rogers first thing in the morning. She is more likely to grunt in your general direction while scratching her armpits or picking her nose. Witty repartee is not in her repertoire. A simple growl usually suffices as pithy conversation both before and after sex. And it tends to be sex in the same old position using the same old ticklers. However, it must be said that what she lacks in creativity, she makes up for in frequency . . . at least before football season begins.

and in conclusion

For loyalty and sensuality, sapphic Bulls are your babe. What they lack in excitement, these majestic women make up for in a healthy interest in sex and unabated generosity. Give her room to spread her warmth and she will reward you with a life filled with beauty and great dinners. She can be stubborn, so expect to raise a white flag rather than wave a red one if she sets her sights on you. Lucky girl!

Alice B. Toklas - April 30

who solidly stood by gertrude stein for decades, feeding her, supporting her and tenaciously attending to her every need? it was the aptly taurean Alice B. Toklas, a world-famous writer in her own right but perhaps better known to the world as the loyal partner to grandstanding gertrude. Dear alice was a typical sapphic Bull: faithful companion, protector, order taker, mastermind of the kitchen and steadfastly loyal lover. what she lacked in stylish flair she amply compensated for in persistence and patience. okay, she wasn't a wild party animal but what taurus is?

relationships with other signs

Taurean girlfriends can go the distance in any relationship. However, before you commit, please check her complete chart. In the meantime, here are simple sun sign comparisons to get you started.

Taurus and Aries—Ram dykes may be too fiery and impetuous for the thoughtful and slow-moving Bull. A successful business partnership is possible because the Bull will be happy to tend to the more mundane tasks while the Ram happily goes out and manifests her destiny. In love, romantic Taurean girlfriends may have their roses trampled and champagne spilled by a Ram stampede to the bedroom. These sensual and steady girls need a slow hand and not a quick romp.

Taurus and Taurus—Two Bulls in one room is either feast or famine. Who will cook and who will clean? Will it be wrestling, football or Xena? Will the vacation be spent sleeping on the couch or in a hammock? Business partnerships may never move forward; love relationships may consist of a romantic evening of beer and bratwurst. Who can tell; they may both like it that way.

Taurus and Gemini—Whether in business or pleasure, the Taurus-Gemini combination will have its share of ups and downs, so be patient and understanding. The sapphic Bull may be too placid for the wired lambda Twin. At the same time, lavender Twins don't have any long-term power of concentration and are apt to be too fickle for the earthy, loyal Taurean woman. Agree to disagree and leave it at that.

Taurus and Cancer—These two women make excellent partners. In both business and love, they are respectful of each other's talents and abilities. Inspirational sapphic Crabs can push the lambda Bull to greater heights and more worthy accomplishments while the Taurean sister gives her warm and fuzzy partner the loyalty she needs. Do I hear the pitter-patter of little claws or hooves?

Taurus and Leo—Committed Taurean dykes provide a good cheering section for the overly dramatic Lion. With constant understanding and patience, they can do well in business by melding the Taurean ability to go the distance and the Leo talent for making things happen. Sadly, in love, the fiery Leo lass may soon tire of the faithful but mundane Bull. What a shame. Leo dykes may learn too late that slow and steady wins the race.

Taurus and Virgo—These two earthy gals are a perfect match for whatever life has to offer. In business, they can run a tidy little firm, using the best qualities of each partner. Both are very detail oriented, loyal and giving. In love, what one disrupts, the other restores. Expect the best of both worlds when these two sapphic sisters join forces and oriforces.

Taurus and Libra—Both Taurus and Libra are ruled by mighty Aphrodite, which means that in many ways they transcend major personality differences and achieve relative harmony and balance. In business, the persevering earthy Bull may be frustrated by the fly-by-night antics of the airy Libra. In love, one gal's fish and chips is the other's *poisson et pommes frites.* An odd couple, if I ever saw one, but they would miss each other if either left.

Taurus and Scorpio—When these two heavenly bodies collide, stand back! In business, they are a formidable pair. The earthy Taurean sister can implement the strategic designs of her Scorpio partner with unmitigated success. In love, the bond is an eternal flame that begins with a raging, uncontrollable fire. See two ninety-year-olds holding hands? Guess their signs.

Taurus and Sagittarius—The sapphic Bull will have to summon more than her usual dollop of patience with the scattered, easily distracted Sag mama. In both business and love, these two mismatched souls may be able to find common ground if they are open and flexible. In many ways, these two are very good for each other, providing fiery excitement where there is earthy lethargy and Bullish beauty where there is Archer filth. Give this match time to grow—like mold.

Taurus and Capricorn—These two practical and earthy girlfriends can create a harmonious and highly successful partnership. In business, these unstoppable bulldozers combine forces and offer stubborn application with careful planning. In love, they can build a sturdy foundation for years of pleasure and security. So it ain't exciting? Whaddaya want?

Taurus and Aquarius—This combination may be stressful. In business, the determination of both women may conflict with each other: Bulls prefer slow and steady doggedness while Aquarians are off and running in the direction that has the greatest lure. In love, one may tire of the other and the other may feel neglected and unloved. Guess who is who.

Taurus and Pisces—While Tauruses are more down to earth, they have a certain innate appeal to spiritual and psychic Piscean mamas. In business, one provides the practical oomph while the other can dream up all sorts of new and wonderful paths. Romance is high on the list in love. These two lambda mamas can generate considerable heat. Pack a thermometer!

famous Tauruses: one a Day

Jessica Lange	actor	April 20
Catherine the Great	empress of Russia	April 21
Vladimir Lenin	revolutionary	April 22
Lee Majors	actor	April 23
Barbra Streisand	performer	April 24
Ella Fitzgerald	singer	April 25
Carol Burnett	actor, comedian	April 26
Sandy Dennis	actor	April 27
Ann-Margret	actor	April 28
Michelle Pfeiffer	actor	April 29
Alice B. Toklas	writer, companion	April 30
Kate Smith	singer	May 1
Bianca Jagger	model	May 2
Niccolò Machiavelli	political philosopher	May 3
Keith Haring	artist	May 4
Karl Marx	revolutionary	May 5
Sigmund Freud	doctor	May 6
Eva Perón	politician, first lady	May 7
Candice Bergen	actor	May 8
Glenda Jackson	actor	May 9
Judith Jamison	dancer	May 10
Salvador Dalí	artist	May 11
Katharine Hepburn	actor	May 12
Bea Arthur	actor	May 13
George Lucas	director	May 14
L. Frank Baum	writer	May 15
Janet Jackson	singer	May 16
Dennis Hopper	actor	May 17
Reggie Jackson	athlete	May 18
Grace Jones	singer, actor	May 19
Cher	performer	May 20

women Born on the cusp

Those born between May 17 and May 23 tend to have a combination of both Taurus and Gemini attributes. The quiet good taste of Taurus matched with the expressiveness of Gemini rewards these sapphic gals with ample creativity, intelligence and eloquence. They are thinkers, inventors and artisans, with the uncanny ability to create something beautiful and utilitarian out of absolute dreck.

Looking for a match to ignite your fire? These gluttonous babes can be easily tempted to overindulge their sexual appetite. Chalk it up to that bullish sensuality mixing with the Twins' enthusiastic fickleness. You may be one of many but, hey, what a ride!

These gals can be crude, lewd and shrewd, depending upon the delicate balance of the earth and air elements in their personal charts. More earthy mamas can become silent Susans, bestowing their filthy comments on only close companions. Airy amazon sisters can dish out the dirt with the best of 'em, in a clever sort of way, to anyone within earshot.

The Twin-Bull is one of the most mercenary women of the zodiac, needing an inordinate amount of money to feel happy and content. Usually she finds a way to satisfy her lusty bottom line by either glomming on to a money honey or winning a high-paying job of her own. However she manages to fill her till, you can bet that she'll find a sweet and sassy lassie to help her spread it around.

The real art of conversation is not only to say the right thing in the right place but to leave unsaid the wrong thing at the tempting moment.
—Dorothy Nevill

Gemini
May 21–June 21
Girl-Girl Twins

Vital Statistics

Element = Air (intellectual, conceptually oriented)

Mode = Mutable (goes with the flow, adapts to change)

Ruling planet = Mercury (the planet of communication, thoughts and talks)

Ruling House = Three (the house of communication, neighborhood, siblings, early education)

Ruling part of the Body = Lungs and arms

Birthstone = Emerald (May) or agate (June)

Best Day = Wednesday

Lucky Number = 3

Astral color = Green, red, blue, white

Flower = Lily of the valley

Tarot card = The Lovers (inquisitive, quick-thinking, adaptive to change)

✿ The wise ancient seers dubbed those born between approximately May 21 and June 21 Gemini the Twins, the third sign of the zodiac.

Perhaps the most famous twins (aside from the Doublemint ones) were Castor and Pollux. They hatched from an egg laid by Leda who was impregnated by a randy Zeus disguised as a randy swan. (This guy gets around!) Castor and Pollux were the guardians of sailors and ostensibly saved ships in distress, although they didn't do a particularly good job with *Titanic*. These twins were inseparable, even in death. When Castor was slain in a war with Idas and Lynceus, Pollux was inconsolable and begged to die in place of his brother. Instead, Zeus allowed the twins to share one life, spending half their time in Hades and half their time on Olympus. They were the first to participate in flextime.

general personality and first impressions

What this means is that sapphic Twins tend to lead double lives. It is not uncommon for them to have two (or more) lovers at one time. They may also hold two jobs, have two homes, two cars, and so on. They are also the masters of opposites, able to see two sides of an argument and have two separate opinions for every issue. (Give me two shots of bourbon; I'm seeing double!)

Gemini dykes have scads of galpals. They are friend to all and, in some respects, close friend to none. They do not like to confide in others, preferring to hide their hurts and quietly heal themselves alone and out of sight. They would rather have you confide your deepest secrets to them, but try to avoid the temptation. They love to gossip and gleefully tell tales. They don't do it to be mean, hurtful or conniving; they just *love* to talk, and what is more interesting than your very personal problems and closely held secrets? Nosy? Her? How'd you guess?

A Gemini can be the life of the party because she is always

"up." Definitely invite at least one sapphic Twin if you are having an intimate dinner gathering; she will keep the conversation flowing with her witty repartee, delightful jokes and gossipy tidbits (especially about the host) to spice things up.

You'll recognize a sapphic Twin by her thin, excitable, somewhat nervous demeanor. She is always on the go and enters a room like a spark of electricity or a bolt of lightning. (Be careful of brush fires.) She can talk a mile a minute and cover a wide range of subjects in the course of a short conversation.

She is very self-conscious and for that reason is one of the fashion hounds of the zodiac. She can wear anything well. Unlike her sloppy sister Sagittarius, Gemini gals have dramatic flair and panache. Expect to see her in the latest styles or in fabulously appointed classics. Scarves, makeup and nylons are not out of the question, although, truth be told, she looks better in tight pants and spikes.

They are always "on" because they yearn to be popular and "in the know." Expect your Gemini woman to be surrounded by a plethora of newly introduced galpals who air-kiss and chitchat at the same time. If you feel a twinge of jealousy seeing her interact with so many attractive babes, don't beat yourself up over it; it's just her nature. Sapphic Twins are known for their flirtatious behavior and wandering eye. They have also been known to tell a fib or two so be warned!

career and work

Because Gemini is the ruler of the third house of communication, neighborhood and early education, sapphic Twins are happiest in careers in which they work with others, exchange ideas and use their agile minds. Don't expect to see them on an assembly line or holed up in a cubicle tallying long lists of numbers all day. They'll go crazy. They are women who need, *ahem,* stimulation

(Don't we all?), and for that reason they gravitate toward professions that bring them into contact with people and ideas. A few possibilities include print or broadcasting, journalism, negotiation, arbitration, teaching and sales. They can reach out to others as well as demonstrate their knowledge and persuasiveness. These sapphic souls are not above playing mind games and may be able to channel some of that excess imagination into inventing something wild and wonderful.

Unlike directed Capricorns, Twin dykes are not corporate plodders, pushers or sweaters. Their attention span is next to nil, they are a bit on the lazy side when it comes to full-fledged sweat equity and they hate routine. However, they are rather adept at sucking up to authority in a charming, nonthreatening way. They are so darned likable and eager to please that sometimes they manage to get a little farther up the corporate food chain than their abilities warrant. In the absence of more sustaining earth signs in their charts (Capricorn, Taurus or Virgo), these girls may have a tendency to fall off Olympus as quickly as they ascended. Thank goodness they are adaptable and generally optimistic; after a quick dusting off, they'll be off on another adventure, on to a new career or just on to a different company. Hey, babe, haven't I seen you someplace before?

This expressive gal may have more than one career in her lifetime. Don't be surprised if she studies one thing in college only to take up with something completely different in the workplace. As with lovers, this woman needs to taste a few different flavors before she finally decides on one.

money

A lesbian Twin is the earn and burn type when it comes to finances. She is far more interested in the excitement of money and what it can buy than in its long-term power and ease. She is also rather generous with her possessions. For these reasons she is apt to squander her payload as fast as she grabs it. Save for a rainy day? Forgetaboutit, sister!

Despite this cavalier attitude, these women manage, through their innate optimism and shmooze-ability, to attract a financial mentor (or lover) and attain some degree of financial success in their lifetime. In time they learn about the importance of saving for retirement but probably not before they look around their house and see a collection of useless junk that they once desperately needed. Hey, love those beanbag chairs and pinup cat posters.

These generous sisters are more than willing to pick up the tab for a party, but they are also the ones who inadvertently leave their wallets at home. Hmmmm. Maybe it's because they are so adamant about being popular that they have a hard time saying no, even when their bottom line sags.

The Gemini Home

Gemini dykes are always on the go and therefore don't put much stock in one permanent abode. Don't be surprised if your Twin moves often, perhaps even across the country and back, in the span of a few years. Chances are she is not currently living in the town where she was born. Like her opposite astrological sister sign, Sagittarius, Gemini sisters live by the credo "Home is where you hang your hat." For those Twins who have a bit more earth in their charts, this energy may result in owning more than one home or living out of a couple of places at once (like a weekend home and a weekday apartment or your place and my place). Misplacing the keys becomes an event!

For all these reasons, Gemini homes tend to look less lived in and like more of a showcase. Sapphic Twins do have an innate sense of design and can make any squalid hellhole a candidate for *Architectural Digest.* (Too claustrophobic? It probably just needs airy curtains . . . or dynamite.)

Her home is primed for communication and will be fitted out with all the latest equipment: computer, phone, fax, whatever it takes to connect with the world. All phones are probably cordless so she can roam and talk at the same time. The look is airy, clean and functional. Forget about overstuffed chairs to snuggle in. If it ain't simple and sleek, you can just stand, sister! And don't even think of moving your trash bin coffee table into the living room.

The kitchen is to die for: clean, functional and state of the art. She is a passable cook when she sets her mind to it, and absolutely *loves* to entertain. The more the merrier! Take a peek at the naked chef, ladies!

Love, sex and Relationships

Old-time astrologers believe that Geminis are unabashedly fickle, uncontrollably flirtatious and have trouble committing to just one woman at a time. Whether this is taken to extremes (Orgy! Orgy!) or not depends upon the placement of other signs and planets in your Twin's horoscope. What is absolutely true is that she will have many, many lovers in her lifetime, many of them simultaneously and many of them probed only in her imagination.

I believe it was Freud who said that most sex is in the mind. That certainly goes for sapphic Twins who cream at the thought of "aural" sex. If she's not turned on to you intellectually, there may not be much physical passion.

But it's not all thought and no action. Physically, Gemini gals are the few truly gifted acrobats in the zodiac, bless their creative little souls. (Ask her to show you the banana trick.) What they lack in stamina, they make up for in enthusiasm, dirty and delicious surprises and sleazy pillow talk. There is no telling what you will find in her box of treats, but eat them quickly before the dessert disappears. If you're looking for a relentless bulldozer, choose a Taurus. For bursts of excitement, your gal is the pink Twin; she likes to double her pleasure and comes in pairs.

With her roving eye, it is easy to understand why she drives some women crazy, especially sensitive, jealous and clinging water signs (Pisces, Cancer and Scorpio). Lesbian Twins can be emotionally distant; they are intellectual but not emotional, physical but not sensual. Maybe that's why they have so much trouble sustaining a monogamous relationship.

To keep your Twin girlfriend from finding lust in other places, leave mysterious, lurid notes for her where she least expects to find them. Whisper delicious little things in her ear. Tell her what you are going to do to her. . . . and make her wait and wait for it. Tickle her with a feather . . . while tying her up . . . then go out to lunch! Distance is an aphrodisiac for these mental acrobats. The secret is to give her plenty of room to roam but slip a sensuous photo of yourself in her wallet, just in case she forgets who you are.

As she gets older, she may consider settling down with one tried and true lover . . . but that crazy notion will soon pass!

friends

Sapphic Twins have many, many proud galpals from all walks of life. She is no snob and is truly interested in other people and what makes them tick. For this reason, you may have to share her attention with the immediate world, but it will be an interesting and rewarding experience. Her gatherings are special events, chockablock with famous and not-so-famous folks exchanging sizzling gossip, bon mots and engaging ideas. You'll find her winding her way through the crowd, whispering in ears and hob-nobbing here and there. Catch her if you can, if only fleetingly, to hear the latest chitchat.

Gemini dykes strive for diversity and diversion, so don't ex-pect a lifetime of dinners for two. More likely you'll have meals on the hoof: a little downtown gathering at 6 P.M. for drinks, fol-lowed by an uptown dinner party at 9 P.M., followed by dessert with "a few" galpals at 11 P.M. Not bad for a Monday.

Proud Twins are not inclined to "get in touch with their feel-ings" or concentrate their efforts on creating a small, intimate circle of friends. Today's close bosom buddy can be tomorrow's also-ran. These airy girls therefore tend to gravitate to those feisty, independent fire signs (Sagittarius, Aries and Leo) or other air signs (Aquarius and Libra) as opposed to clingy, sensitive, jealous water signs (Cancer, Scorpio and Pisces) or sedate, home-loving earth signs (Taurus, Virgo and Capricorn).

family and parents

A Lesbian Twin tends to get along well with most family members. This is because she can't abide bigotry and narrow-mindedness and would cut off communication with any relative who did not unconditionally accept her for who she is. She is an independent soul who doesn't particularly care what others think, especially when it curtails her freedom and self-affirmation.

Because of her verbal agility and restless persona, she proba-bly came out, proud and queer, early in life. There is a time and a place for mind games in her life, but this is not it. In perhaps one of the few instances of pure, unadulterated honesty, she will an-nounce her sexual orientation to her family and let the chips fall where they may. Intolerant types won't have this babe to kick around anymore. She'll tell them to keep their lousy homemade Christmas presents. "I'm off to Paris with my lovergrrl!"

As a child, this girl had an overwhelming need to fit in and have loads of friends. Wise and understanding parents understood this and did not begrudge her a trendy wardrobe or an occasional faddish trinket that she had to have to impress and belong. They also allowed her to throw a few parties now and then and welcomed countless packs of galpals for milk and cookies. Hopefully they would have recognized her restless, imaginative nature and gave her plenty of space both physically and mentally.

communication style

Sapphic Twins are expressive and witty souls. They are high on intellect and pride themselves on being in the know, with all the hot news and notable noteworthies. They can be very chatty and informative but also tend to have rather short attention spans. If your Twin appears unfocused, chalk it up to an active mind gravitating to a new subject because the current one is too darn boring!

Like steadfast Taurus, this sapphic sister does not tend to dredge up emotional nuclear waste to win an argument. That is all too heavy and destructive for the chatty, friendly Twin. Let's leave the verbal pyrotechnics to fiery-lipped Sagittarius or vengeful Scorpio. The best way to win an argument with this gal is to let her think she's right. Fairly soon after that, she'll be off on another little tangent and will forget what the bickering was about anyway.

Health and fitness

Lesbian Twins have high nervous energy that can carry them short distances very quickly. However, they are not especially good for the long haul, either tending to lose interest, energy or direction. It is for this reason that they do best with a personal trainer who can keep them on track and on schedule. Their greatest day-to-day challenge is the proper channeling of their considerable energy. Constant fatigue, eye strain, headaches and general dissipation and waste are some of the most crushing chronic ailments that can befall a Twin sister. But I suppose it can always be worse . . .

Because Gemini rules the lungs and arms, amazon Twins should be particularly careful of lung or respiratory infections or activity that can damage their arms, like skiing. (Hugging, however, is always safe.) Damage to these areas can really bog them down and they may take a while to fully recuperate.

Gemini women tend to have wiry frames, may have trouble putting on weight and tend to remain on the thin side throughout their life. All that nervous, slimming energy can burn off the calories like a stoking, toking furnace. The sexiest part of their body is most likely their well-developed arms—all the better to wrap around you! Yikes!

shhh—secrets and fears

What's lurking in the astrological closets of a queer Twin? The areas of her solar chart that contain feelings of guilt, repression, ancestral baggage or family pressure are ruled by sedate earth signs. Outwardly, she is a sexually carefree spirit, unable to be captured and tied down (well, maybe tied down occasionally), but in those dark recesses of her psyche she yearns for stability and loyalty. It's fine for her to flit from clit to clit, but it would depress and distress her if her partner did the same. There is no sauce for the goose with this saucy girl. Spiritually, she is not as wildly ecumenical as she appears. In fact, left to her own deeply submerged devices, she can become pedantic and, dare I say, closeminded. When it comes to her family, she really does want approval from Mom and Dad, even though she would vehemently deny it if asked. Deny! Deny! Deny! I don't want to talk about it. And she can be downright stubborn about it.

They are also terribly afraid of being out of the loop of communication. Do you mean to say that a new fad is on the scene and I didn't know about it? Impossible!

weaknesses: are there any?
Of course there are weaknesses. Every sign has a seamy side, cousin, but we astrologers like to call them "character builders." These woman have a small litany of weak spots. Aside from being branded shallow, two-faced, lying and fickle, these feisty gals may also be tempted to sexual extremes. It is no coincidence that the Marquis de Sade was a Gemini, among other things. Ouch! 'Nuf said, girlfriend.

In any project, social situation or business venture, there must always be something in it for them or they will make themselves scarce. Their agile minds are always figuring out if the odds are in their favor before they commit or expend energy. Other more self-sacrificing signs, like Virgo, may despair of Gemini's fair-weather assistance, but if you can convince her that there is something, anything, in it for her, this sapphic Twin will give it her all with the best of them.

and in conclusion
If you want a trip to the moon on gossamer wings, book a flight on a sapphic Twin. She is a woman of excitement and savoir faire who can get you beyond the velvet ropes of any hoity-toity club or into the back room at any high-level affair. In fact, with her

charm and grace, she can get you just about anywhere! For sheer fun, pluck this rosy woman from the bunch and water her in your bud vase.

Sandra Bernhard - June 6

They say sapphic Twins are chatty, clever, witty and highly wired. come to think of it, they say these things about the sapphic sandra Bernhard. coincidence? I think not. comedian sandra is in the perfect profession for a gemini: where else can you get paid for mouthing off? (extra bonus: You can also hang out with other celebrities and get your gossip firsthand instead of scouring the tabloids.) They say gemini are fickle in love and have trouble settling down with just one lovergrrl. 'Nuf said.

Relationships with other signs

Lesbian Gemini are tempted to try any combination, but I advise you to check her entire chart first. Impatient gals can quickly peruse the following sun sign compatibilities for a general outlook.

Gemini and Aries—These two women create quite a pair in both love and business partnerships. Both are independent and energetic but in different, complementary ways: Sapphic Twins are more intellectual and lambda Rams are more physical. Love relationships can be passionate, but the flame can die out quickly. To keep the fires burning, keep a supply of whipped cream and silk scarves on hand.

Gemini and Taurus—The Gemini-Taurus combination whether in business or pleasure will have its share of ups and downs, so be patient and understanding. The intellectual Twin may be too nerve-racking for the sedate sapphic Bull. At the same time, lavender Twins have a wandering eye and are apt to be too fickle for the earthy, loyal Taurean woman. Agree to disagree and leave it at that.

Gemini and Gemini—When two Twins get together they can either double their pleasure or double their agita. In business, they may never come to terms on the direction of a company or project, both preferring to be the out-front spokeswoman and not the back-office drone. In love, it may be like two ships passing in the night as both attend to their respective social circles. But when these two heavenly bodies collide, it is an incredible sight to behold!

Gemini and Cancer—Business partnerships between these two divergent souls have a better chance of success than love matches. In business, one expands the business vision while the other dutifully maintains the back office. In love, the Crab dyke may demand more attention than her lovergrrl is prepared to give. Emotionally, lesbian Twins are simply too flirtatious and fickle for the committed Cancer. If only the Crab would rouge her nipples on occasion.

Gemini and Leo—The feisty combination of these two independent sisters works better in business than it does in love. The easily distracted Twin can be kept in line by the ferociously fiery Leo lass. Much can be accomplished when each one brings out the best in the other. In love, Gemini dykes may tire of Leo's ongoing desire to be numero uno, and lambda Lions may not cotton to the Twin's wandering appetite. The problem is that Gemini cannot eat Lion every night!

Gemini and Virgo—Both of these mutable gals are ruled by thoughtful Mercury so at the very least, there will be a meeting of the minds when Gemini and Virgo lesbians get together. In business, they are excellent partners, each providing a unique set of talents and abilities to the process. In love, Virgos are able to philosophize about their Gemini lovergrrl's shortcomings, while the sapphic Twin can give her Virginal partner something to obsess about.

Gemini and Libra—These two airy girlfriends have an instant attraction, but are there long-term possibilities? In business, neither one is content to tend to the nitty-gritty day-to-day details. However, in love, these two seem to know instinctively what turns the other on. Suggestion: Hire a troop of earthy gals to run the office and work instead on your . . . market positioning.

Gemini and Scorpio—How long will the fickle Gemini gal survive partnered with the vengeful and suspicious Scorpio sister? Love relationships may never get off the ground . . . or the couch . . . or the patio chair. But there is more to a partnership than just sex, sex, sex. In business, what may begin as an equal partnership may eventually evolve into Gemini serfdom. Is Scorpio a stern taskmistress? Ouch!

Gemini and Sagittarius—On the one hand a partnership between these two babes is based on absolute equality and mutual understanding. It is the perfect business arrangement. On the other hand, would there be enough passion between them to sustain a long-term love match? I don't know. I suppose you could try.

Gemini and Capricorn—Enthusiastic but wandering queer Twins may be reined in by serious sapphic Caps. This provides potential for success in business but can be hell in love. At work, the Goat gal keeps things on an even keel while the expressive Twin expands the corporate vision. In love, it would be like living with your sixth grade teacher. How much did you enjoy sixth grade?

Gemini and Aquarius—The airy combination of Gemini and Aquarius works well in both business and pleasure. In business, the exuberance of Gemini gals can push the Aqueerian to greater and greater feats of daring. In love, both women are expressive and excitable. The meeting of two great air masses can create a tornado. Hunker down and enjoy it.

Gemini and Pisces—Sapphic Twins are too independent for the loyal and sensitive rainbow Fish. In business, both are too impractical to get anything of substance going. In love, the initial attraction soon gives way to the realization that each woman wants something different out of the relationship. That's the way it goes.

famous geminis: one a day

Jeffrey Dahmer	cannibal, murderer	May 21
Naomi Campbell	model	May 22
Joan Collins	actor	May 23
Patti La Belle	singer	May 24
Anne Heche	actor	May 25
Sally Ride	astronaut	May 26
Isadora Duncan	dancer, choreographer	May 27
Gladys Knight	singer	May 28
Melissa Etheridge	singer, songwriter	May 29
Christine Jorgensen	transsexual	May 30
Brooke Shields	model, actor	May 31
Marilyn Monroe	actor	June 1
Marquis de Sade	writer	June 2
Josephine Baker	performer	June 3
Rosalind Russell	actor	June 4
Laurie Anderson	performance artist	June 5
Sandra Bernhard	comedian	June 6
Artist Formerly Known as Prince	performer	June 7
Barbara Bush	first lady	June 8
Cole Porter	composer	June 9
Judy Garland	performer	June 10
Adrienne Barbeau	actor	June 11
George Bush	politician, president	June 12
Ally Sheedy	actor	June 13
Margaret Bourke-White	photographer	June 14
Xaviera Hollander	madam, writer	June 15
Katharine Graham	publisher	June 16
Anastasia	royal	June 17
Isabella Rossellini	actor	June 18
Kathleen Turner	actor	June 19
Cyndi Lauper	singer	June 20
Dianne Feinstein	politician, senator	June 21

women born on the cusp

Those born between June 19 and June 24 tend to have a combination of both Gemini and Cancer attributes.

These sapphic gals are the quintessential bon vivants, mixing Gemini vitality and generosity with Cancerian love of affection. This delightful combination of spunk and spark helps them enlist helpful galpals and comrades in arms from all corners of the world.

Mutable Gemini go with the cosmic flow, while the cardinal Crab energy often pushes for change just for the sake of change. The combination of these two excitable energies makes this Twin-Crab a go-getter without necessarily a sense of direction. It can also make her somewhat of a procrastinator, trying to choose one course of action over another and eventually doing nothing in all the confusion.

These doting mamas have an almost excessive love of children and may push and push partners until they have a few of their own. They are kind but also opinionated and are not particularly directed or self-disciplined. What they lack in oomph and followthrough, they make up for in charm, grace, sex appeal and homeyness. They are also rather good cooks. Have a bite of my hot apple pie.

The best and most beautiful things in the
world cannot be seen or even touched.
They must be felt with the heart.
—Helen Keller

*

cancer
June 22–July 22
Steamy Crabs

Vital Statistics

Element = water (fluid, emotionally oriented)

Mode = cardinal (conceives of and creates change)

Ruling planet = Moon (the planet of emotions, estrogen and mother)

Ruling house = fourth (the house of privacy and security issues, home life, family)

Ruling part of the body = breasts and stomach

Birthstone = Agate (June) or ruby (July)

Best Day = Monday

Lucky number = 4

Astral color = pink, green, reddish brown

Flower = Rose

Tarot card = The chariot (protection, safeguard, victory and success)

The wise ancient seers dubbed those born between approximately June 22 and July 22 Cancer the Crab, the fourth sign of the zodiac.

Diana (the Moon) was always pegged as a cold virgin. What the chauvinistic experts didn't know was that she was capable of great, unbridled passion. As it turned out, Endymion, a husky shepherd with not much to say, sparked and stoked that passion. The Moon fell in love with him, but rather than declare her love she decided to avoid possible rejection; she sent him into a perpetual slumber so she could keep tabs on him and have him all to herself. Every night she would come down from the heavens for kisses, caresses and some cheap thrills, confident in the knowledge that she was the only one in his life. She also tended his sheep and they flourished very nicely without him. Talk about a compulsive, possessive woman!

general personality and first impressions

Mama mia! If Diana the Moon sounds like a woman desperate for unconditional love, make a mental note of Cancer the Crab, which is the sign that is ruled by the moon. Also note the symbolism of the Crab, which is a hard-shelled creature with a soft, mushy, vulnerable center. These Crabby women tend to have a crusty, hard-to-get-to-know exterior that belies a warm, soft and downright cuddly inner core. Sapphic Crabs are arguably the smotheringest, motheringest women of the zodiac. So don't be put off by the severe exterior; it's worth getting to know her a bit better, cracking her hard shell and tasting her sweet meat.

Old-time astrologers noted that Cancers embody all the attributes of a woman. But don't get too excited, sisters; these historical attributes are not on my hit parade of most flattering personal traits. Check a few of these out: moody, compulsive, clinging, timid, weak, dreamy, false, nosy, whiney, traditional, conservative, smothering, nagging, yadda, yadda, yadda. Heck, what do these old bachelors know about women anyway? I prefer to say that sapphic Cancers can be described as courageous, intuitive, sympathetic, maternal, sensitive, protective, strong, determined, productive, procreative, psychic, tuned in to feelings and giving. Now that's what I call a woman! Okay, let's face it, at times she can be a bit overly sensitive and clingy too.

You can recognize a typical Crab by her conservative demeanor. In a roomful of radical dykes wearing nothing but bellybutton studs and last night's spaghetti sauce, she's the one in the dirndl and sensible shoes. Genetics always plays a role in appearance, but generally speaking she will be on the pale side with a moon-shaped face and large, expressive eyes. When you look up *fem* in the dictionary, chances are you'll see a Cancer gal peering back at you with moist eyes and lips.

Don't try to put something over on her, unless it's your leg; she is one of those intuitive water signs who can sense if you are not being totally truthful. And, oh, how you'll pay and pay and pay!

career and work
Because Cancer is the ruler of the fourth house of home, hearth and personal security, expect to see your Crab mama in the more nurturing, so-called female-oriented occupations such as nurse, gynecologist, hospice or daycare worker, teacher (especially nursery or kindergarten), flight attendant or cook. Because she is the first of the water signs, she may make her watermark in liquid areas such as milk, bottled water or other beverage production. John the Baptist was a Cancer, in case you want to know.

She is not one for rough-and-tumble politics or acerbic and strategic corporate maneuvering. We leave that to politically motivated Scorpios or strategically conniving Gemini. Crab sisters couldn't foresee a professional opportunity if they were swallowed up by it. Their ultimate success is based upon hard sweat equity that is hopefully recognized within their career lifetimes. Unlike vainglorious Leos, Cancer dykes are not terribly interested in getting credit for every little thing they do. These lovely ladies subscribe to the ethic "Hard work brings its own rewards." Theirs is a behind-the-scenes, don't make waves, old-fashioned attitude toward their jobs. In the worst-case scenario, your Crab may be out of step with the vagaries of today's corrupt corporate jungle and may be eaten up by the machine. Best-case scenario: She falls in with the right company and becomes the indispensible mascot of the office. Happily, because she is modest, persevering and patient, she tends to survive even the most destructive corporate onslaughts.

If she does make a run for political office expect to see her name listed to the right of the political spectrum. At heart, she simply fears change and the unknown. She is a patriot who prefers the nostalgic good old days of safe streets and clean front yards. (I wonder if she also remembers life in the closet.) Though personally it never ceases to amaze me that there are women who are anti-choice, these Crab dolls tend to be among them. Chalk it up to their overwhelming maternal instinct and don't get into a long discussion about it. Don't promise her your vote; you may regret it.

money

A sapphic Crab is a clever gal when it comes to money management. She has an innate ability to make a little bit of money go a long, long way and tends to earn it in little bits and pieces from many small transactions just like a shopkeeper or a waitress. She is not a wheeler-dealer stock-market trader with her stash, however, preferring to put her money where it is safe. The bank with a rousing 2 percent fully taxable interest is good enough for her, thank you very much!

She is forever plagued by the fear of destitution, logical or not. Stories of old ladies living hand to mouth despite hefty bank balances could be an amazon Crab life story. Try to be understanding when she travels from store to store to save an extra twenty-five cents or when she buys generic laundry detergent and reduced-price, slightly dented canned goods. She is an incurable bargain hunter who tries to make every penny spend like a dime. At the most extreme, there are those sapphic Crabs who enjoy an afternoon of poking through the public garbage in search of deposit bottles and cans. Hey, I just made fifteen cents!

Through all of this, she is not an especially greedy or conniving person. Unlike sneaky Scorps, she is not particularly interested in cheating anybody out of their just due. She only wants to assure a worry-free old age where she can buy anything she wants (with all the anticipated applied discounts) anytime she wants. Is that so wrong?

The cancer Home

If you are claustrophobic, hold your breath and brace yourself before you enter a lesbian Crab's home. It is chockablock with knickknacks, dust collectors and assorted treacly junk. Cluttered doesn't even begin to describe the scene; it's almost womblike. However, unlike filthy and lazy Sagittarians, these Crab babes know how to dust and keep a clean and tidy home. They know that potpourri alone won't cover up food smells. Ya gotta scrub a dub, bub!

Sapphic Crabs tend to prefer early-American furnishings and don't spare the chintz. They gravitate toward the old-fashioned homey look of overstuffed chairs, billowy curtains, pillows galore and an understated home-entertainment center. Your Crab may still use a record player or eight-track that she bought at a thrift shop years ago. Hey, it still works!

Her well-appointed kitchen is the center of activity. She *loves* to cook and, as she gets older, she looks like it. Look to her for the old standards: pot roast, mashed potatoes, chicken potpie, meat loaf, apple cobbler . . . I feel stuffed already. Fey nouvelle cuisine is not in her repertoire, honey buns.

ʟoue, sex and ʀelationships

Old-time astrologers say that Cancerian women tend to be the mothering type, which conjures up all sorts of Oedipal scenarios for their lovergrrls. Fact is, sisters, these gals just simply *love* to play house and don't necessarily care about who plays the nurturing mama and who plays the hungry babe. But she is more affectionate than passionate. Cancer rules the breasts and the stomach, which warms my heart. Sapphic Crabs tend to have ample, warm and generous breasts (the better to snuggle you, my dear) and love to feed (and overfeed) their partners. Combine the best of both worlds and simply nibble on her breasts whenever you can.

While she is not as possessive as other water signs (Scorpio and Pisces), she is highly sensitive and craves constant affirmation. Think twice before you take her to your local hotspot, park her by the bar and go off to schmooze. Chances are you'll come home to a chilly reception, a cold bed and no supper. And no spanking either, bad girl! She demands every ounce of your love and will withdraw into a sulk if she feels demeaned and ignored. (It's better than all that Aries yelling, I suppose.) This closeness works well with other highly emotional water signs (Scorpio and Pisces) but strangles the life out of the fiercely independent fire signs (Aries, Sagittarius and Leo). Water douses fire, after all.

If you've ever thought of starting a family, consider pairing up with a Crab gal. She's the one who would give up her career (such that it is) to raise the little mites and will always have a hot meal waiting for you when you return home after a hard day fighting dragons. Turkey baster, anyone?

friends

Sapphic Crabs tend to have a very small circle of bosom buddies and trusted family members. She is not a bon vivant like perky Gemini and is not able to work a room like charismatic Libra. Hers is an intimate gathering of longtime soul friends who share the same values and outlooks on life. In a large crowded party full of strangers, she'll be the one sitting in the far corner either clinging to the only person she knows or sitting pathetically alone waiting for someone, anyone, to talk to her. You may also find her parked by the food, providing trenchant epicurean commentary to whomever will listen as she stuffs her face with finger food. (Anyone I know?)

Once you gain entrance into her exclusive club, she is your galpal forever. She will stick by you through thick and thin, putting up with all your life's ups and downs and even making you feel better about being such a loser. She is one of the most loyal women in the zodiac, even to those annoying Sagittarians who drip chocolate sauce on her white couch then try to lick it up with their tongues.

family and parents

Unless there are some harsh aspects in her chart, sapphic Crabs tend to be very close to their relatives, abiding untold hurts and cruelties with stoicism and grace. No matter what, they never forget a birthday or an anniversary and are avid participants in any genealogical expedition. (Hey, didn't I see you on the *Mayflower?)* It may take several years longer than usual for this woman to leave the family bosom and seek another quite a bit more affirming, warm and sexy. Fact is, she may actually enjoy staying close to home despite its possible restrictions and homophobic prejudices because she feels it is "safe." My advice, sister: Buy a security blanket instead!

She is there when her parents or siblings need her, no matter how unsupportive they might have been throughout her life. While I don't like to think of her as a doormat, that moniker may have a ring of truth to it only because the concept of family is so overarchingly important to her. The worst cases are those sad types who never fully come out of the closet and instead live out the best years of their lives tending to mother in her old age. Thankfully though, these particular Cancerian sisters are getting harder and harder to find. Thank goodness for proud modern women.

Lesbian Crabs tended to be girlie girls who never really liked to roll in the mud, climb trees, build forts or eat insects. These delicate young things probably sat on the sidelines in frilly white anklettes and moist underpants quietly eyeing the other girls having rollicking good times. She was probably the teacher's pet, which never earned her popularity points and almost guaranteed a periodic thrashing from jealous Aries girls. However, the clever Crab dyke eventually wised up and recruited a robust Aries as her personal protector. A fool she is not!

communication style

Crab sisters are more reticent than most women but don't think for a minute that they are unable to say what's on their minds. Fact is, they are quite adept at getting their point across and are fairly diplomatic in the process. They have the common touch, blessed with the uncanny ability to relate to practically anyone no matter how high (or low) their station or circumstance. They'll even talk to Scorpios! For this reason, Cancer dykes generally get what they want when they want it. Don't underestimate this sister; you'll wind up the loser.

Some less-charitable astrologers refer to lesbian Crabs as the perfect example of naggy, manipulative whiners, but I'd rather say that they are uniquely expressive individuals who can plumb the depths of human emotion when necessary. They are also not above digging up the dirt and happily examining the dark underbelly of celebrity life. They simply adore gossipy biographies—the more lurid the better!

Health and Fitness

Sapphic Crabs are generally not thought of as robust because they are not as athletically inclined as other women. Instead of running a few laps every day or perhaps lifting weights, they prefer to lap other things and lift a few beers at a favorite dyke site. Instead of rock and rolling the night away, they prefer a quiet evening at home cocooning, relaxing and nibbling. This general inactivity contributes to an overall delicate constitution, sluggishness and a tendency to be overweight. Hey, but then there's just more of her to love! She has absolutely no willpower in the eating department. Remember, if it's on the table, it's in her mouth, so if you want to get her attention, get on the table.

For all of the above reasons, she doesn't bounce back quickly from infections or colds. So, if you really care for her, you will try to get her off her butt and get a little sweat on her brow. (Okay, okay, there may be ways of bringing on the sweat without getting her off her butt.) In all seriousness, she needs to strengthen her constitution through exercise, so, if you really love her, don't allow her to become too lazy, sedate or lethargic. Tempt her with a workout after she works out.

shhh—secrets and fears

Here are the closeted secrets about sapphic Crabs: The areas of her solar chart that contain feelings of guilt, repression, ancestral baggage or family pressure are ruled by flighty air signs. This means that, despite all outward appearances of deep emotional engagement, the Cancer woman secretly yearns to distance herself from ties that bind, especially with unaffirming family members. But how can she do this without feeling like she is a selfish bitch? Inwardly, she is a helium balloon waiting to be released in a blast of freedom and liberation.

Sexually, this sister may be less monogamous than she lets on and secretly wants to pick and choose from a variety of unusual and unorthodox lovergrrls like an open buffet. She may be pretty off the wall herself. What would partners say if she dyed her pubic hair lavender . . . or shaved it all off? Yikes! Or maybe she really seeks a hot tomato rather than a platonic galpal for a life partner?

Spiritually she is more eclectic, ecumenical and experimental than you may think, but she imagines her deepest urges and extreme beliefs to be like a Pandora's box that, once opened, unleashes untold problems as well as a bunch of nasty, poisonous snakes. Hmmmm, that's not Pandora's box that I carefully examined, poked and tasted!

Don't buttonhole her to explain these secret areas. She would curl up and die of embarrassment before she would admit to any of these left-field thoughts and feelings. However, somewhere in the back of her satin undies drawer is a tube of lavender hair dye and a curling iron. Hey, you never know.

weaknesses: are There any?

Let's refer to them simply as "character builders," shall we? At worst, Crab dykes play the long-suffering little woman who stoically puts up with her philandering lovergrrl. Ah, if only she would *quietly* suffer though! Not our little Ms. Saint. Piss and moan, piss and moan. The world has to know how patient and loyal she is and how horrible and selfish her partner is. She can also be charged with emotional manipulation. Who can resist those soulful weepy eyes full of accusation and hurt staring back at you after you've strayed? Only an Aquarian, obviously.

She can also be overly sensitive to the point that you only have to breathe in the wrong direction and she'll get upset. Try walking on eggshells instead; there is less to crush. Independent women such as those with air (Gemini, Libra or Aquarius) or fire (Sagittarius, Leo or Aries) unintentionally crush this hothouse orchid on a regular basis. Remember though, the long-term viability of a love match between Cancers and the air or fire signs depends upon other planets in each woman's horoscope.

and in conclusion

If your interest is in romance, a faithful heart and a home-cooked meal, cast your vote for a lambda Crab. You will be her blue plate special when everyone else considers you roadkill, and she can offer you years (and years and years) of love, affection and companionship. Life would be harsh, lonely and cold without her.

Princess Diana - July 1

There was something about gay-friendly Diana that conjured up all sorts of cancerian traits—mothering, vulnerable, sensitive and seeking unconditional love. As she honed her royal skills, she was able to demonstrate her determined, productive and sympathetic side despite her clashes with the monarchy's political machine. In a life cut too short, she attained a reputation as a caring, sensitive woman whose compassion touched us all—lesbian, gay, straight and all rainbow colors in between. Guess her sign, sisters.

Relationships with other signs

Before you commit to anyone, examine her entire horoscope. In the meantime check out these sun sign compatibilities, but take it all with a grain of salt.

Cancer and Aries—Mighty Aphrodite Aries tears at the delicate emotional seams of a sapphic Cancer gal. Business partnerships can be stressful as the aggressive lambda Ram creates tension and worry for the mild-mannered lesbian Crab. In love, Mother Cancer is willing to serve and aching to nurture. The amazon Aries is willing to be served but can't be restrained. Okay, maybe with leather straps.

Cancer and Taurus—Hard-working lambda Crabs and determined sapphic Bulls make an unbeatable pair in both business and in love. They are in sync emotionally and committed to the success of any proud enterprise. Inspired sapphic Crabs can push the lambda Bull to achieve her heart's desires, while the Taurean mama gives her Cancer gal the support and affection she craves. Do I smell surf and turf?

Cancer and Gemini—If these two are ever going to get together, compromises will have to be made. Sapphic Twins are too cavalier for emotional Crabs. In business, one will happily wander off to meet and greet while the other fretfully stays at the office to open the mail and answer the phone. In love, the lavender Crab may demand more attention than the Twin dyke is prepared to give. Perhaps if she put a little honey in her pot, her Gemini lovergrrl would get her hand stuck.

Cancer and Cancer—When two Crabs get together they can either spend their time building something together or pissing and moaning about it. In business, neither of them may feel comfortable being the pioneer to drum up new business, but they can do very well maintaining a well-functioning enterprise. In love, both want the full attention of the other, and they may just get it!

Cancer and Leo—The Cancer-Leo combination may work well in business, where lambda Leos are anxious to promote and enlarge while sapphic Crabs are content to manage and maintain. In love, the queer Cancer mama would be expected to defer to her perennially proud Lion in just about everything. How does that sit with you, Crabby lovergrrl?

Cancer and Virgo—Here is a great meeting of the minds. The Cancer-Virgo combination is unbeatable in both business and love. Both women have a practical stick-to-itiveness and recognize the importance of maintaining mutual effort to celebrate the good and overcome the bad times. Cleanliness is next to godliness with these two pristine Pamelas, unless of course chocolate sauce is involved.

Cancer and Libra—Crabby, concerned Cancer gals may nip at the heels of carefree lesbian Libras. In business, the sapphic Crab does the filing and makes the coffee while the breezy Libra lunches with her so-called clients. In love, guess who sits up all night waiting with a cold dinner for you-know-who to come sauntering in? No names, please!

Cancer and Scorpio—These two deeply emotional mamas can move mountains in both business and pleasure. While the Crab dyke tends to the structural day-to-day needs of the office, the strategic Scorp sister plans world domination and manifests her corporate destiny. Sexually, these two mamas can steam the room with their passion. Is a hot and spicy platter of seafood fra diavolo on the menu?

Cancer and Sagittarius—The sensitive Crab may have her best moves thwarted by the rollickingly clumsy Sag gal. However, in business, these two gals have a good balance of stability and oomph. One will cause a rumpus while the other sweeps up the mess. In love, however, the down-to-earth Archer technique may be off-putting to the sensitive and romantic Crab. No, I don't want a bite of your postcoital hotdog!

Cancer and Capricorn—The Cancer-Capricorn combination can work well in both business and pleasure. These two conservative, dedicated souls support each other's efforts and bolster each other's egos. In love, each one gives and demands loyalty. Even the sex is mutually pleasing. Sounds like a good deal to me!

Cancer and Aquarius—Crab mamas may be too overprotective for independent no-holds-barred Aquarians who hate being questioned on their every little move. In business, one is happy to stay in the office and keep things on track while the other beats the bushes. In love, one's undying love and devotion is the other's suffocation. Let's face it, Aqueerians hate being tied down . . . most of the time.

Cancer and Pisces—This highly romantic combination makes for a lovey-dovey pair of birds. Even in business they seem to know exactly what the other one is thinking and will do what they can to make things a success. In love, there is such a meeting of the minds and bodies that you couldn't get a crowbar to pry these two apart. Some gals have all the luck!

famous cancers: one a day

Meryl Streep	actor	June 22
Wilma Rudolph	athlete	June 23
John the Baptist	mystic	June 24
George Orwell	writer	June 25
Babe Zaharias	athlete	June 26
Emma Goldman	revolutionary	June 27
Kathy Bates	actor	June 28
Stokely Carmichael	activist	June 29
Lena Horne	singer	June 30
Princess Diana	royal	July 1
Imelda Marcos	first lady	July 2
Gloria Allred	lawyer, feminist	July 3
Gina Lollobrigida	actor	July 4
Eliot Feld	choreographer	July 5
Nancy Reagan	first lady	July 6
Shelly Duvall	actor	July 7
Angelica Huston	actor	July 8
Tom Hanks	actor	July 9
Virginia Wade	athlete	July 10
Kristy Yamaguchi	athlete	July 11
Richard Simmons	fitness personality	July 12
Harrison Ford	actor	July 13
Woody Guthrie	singer	July 14
Linda Ronstadt	singer	July 15
Ginger Rogers	dancer	July 16
Phyllis Diller	comedian	July 17
Nelson Mandela	activist, president	July 18
Lizzie Borden	suspected murderer	July 19
Diana Rigg	actor	July 20
Robin Williams	actor	July 21
Emily Saliers	singer	July 22

women born on the cusp

Those born between July 19 and July 25 tend to have a combination of both Cancer and Leo attributes.

Don't stand in the way of a Crabby Lion. These women are ambitious and covetous with the ability to set their sights on a particular goal and, by dint of intellectual superiority alone, easily attain it. She is a master of mindgames and craves excitement—the more recklessly thrilling the better. She was probably the first one to volunteer to bungee-jump into a craggy cavern or skydive out of a perfectly good airplane. And she is quite dexterous: Ever hear of the "mile high" club? She discovered the "mile down" club.

In the most optimal combination of strengths, she'll have the Cancerian ability to preach to the masses and the Leo talent for self-promotion, resulting in one of the most successful political animals you'll ever meet. She also may be blessed with a good memory and intensely loyal bosom buddies.

On the downside, she tends to demand absolute loyalty but is not always prepared to reciprocate. To keep her eye on your prize, feed the Lion in her by spoiling her mercilessly. She *loves* luxury so be luxurious.

nothing exceeds like excess.
—oscar wilde

Leo

July 23–August 22
The Drama Queen

Vital Statistics

Element = Fire (energetic, action oriented)

Mode = fixed (fights change, attempts stability)

Ruling planet = sun (the planet of the life force, happiness, self-actualization)

Ruling House = fifth (the house of fun, creativity, the arts—especially theater, romance, children)

Ruling part of the body = Heart

Birthstone = Ruby (July) or onyx (August)

Best Day = sunday

Lucky Number = 5

Astral color = yellow, red, green

flower = Larkspur

Tarot card = strength VIII (exerts great energy, attains success through great struggle)

The wise ancient seers dubbed those born between approximately July 23 and August 22 Leo the Lion, the fifth sign of the zodiac.

When I think of the fire sign of Leo and its ruling planet the sun, I can't help but think of the angel Uriel from Jewish mythology. Uriel isn't just any old angel with a couple of wings and a harp. This particular putti is an archangel and the leader of the entire angelic army, so you can only imagine. Uriel is better known as the angel of light who manifests himself as a hungry lion who consumes our sacrificial carcasses at the fiery altar of the Temple. Yummy. Come on, Leo the Lion, with your fiery sun ruler; light my fire and consume me!

general personality and first impressions

Grrrrrrr. This hot image of some ravenously regal fiery lion (a.k.a. the king of beasts) fits rather nicely with the burning personality profile of the lambda Leo. Like Sagittarius, the half human—half horse Centaur, Leo the Lion has a bit of the feisty animal in her. She cannot be reined in (unless you're talking silk scarves around the bedpost) and she enjoys being the center of attention . . . or else! Look up benevolent dictator in the dictionary and you'll see her photo.

Many astrology books indicate that Leo gals have a literal lionlike mane of hair that may be uncontrollably thick and wavy but exceedingly sexy and bold. She prefers to wear her hair au naturale either in a cascading mass or deliciously short and sweet. Like a lion, she carries herself regally. However, despite her need to outshine others, she tends to spend relatively little time on her physical appearance. That's because she knows that she is naturally debonair, sexy and magnanimous *(ahem!).* Hey, sometimes personality alone is alluringly magnetic, babe! Her first priority is to be adored and admired. Barring that, she accepts simply being enviously noticed.

Expect your Lion to be surrounded by a bevy of admiring gal-pals who hang on her every word. This is not just because she is superlative and generous but also because she is so darn nice and gracious. Unlike overly sensitive water signs (Pisces, Cancer and the ever-vengeful Scorpio), Leo gals are trusting, forgiving and understanding. Stab her in the back and she will heal, double-cross her and she will regain her footing and soon forget. But don't think of her as a punching bag; there will come a time when she will lose patience and take a good bite out of your hide as any self-respecting Lion would. Hey, then forgive and forget, right?

There is a part of her that is a petulant baby; she demands authority and attention and will sulk off if not given the recognition and power she feels she so rightly deserves. After all, someone has to lead the pride parade and it might as well be her since she is simply the best. It's not a question of ego, it's just a fact. All right?

career and work

Most sapphic Leos secretly aspire to royalty but in most democratic societies they don't have that option. However, whatever line of work Leo dykes gravitate toward, inevitably they strive for the job of boss. In a restaurant she would have to be the head chef or owner; in a school, the principal; in a newspaper, the publisher; in a corporation, the CEO; in astrology, the star—you get the idea.

They also make excellent divas, striving for centerstage with its adoring crowds. They are also pioneers in their respective fields, independently and stubbornly forging ahead and conquering new territory that they can rule. Whether it's feminist

Eleanor Smeal or pistol-packing Annie Oakley, Leo women are profound forces of change with whom to be reckoned.

I wouldn't be surprised if a young amazon Lion dreamed of being a great actor or a rock and roll star with adoring teeny-bopper fans. More than likely, she spent hour upon hour posing and performing in front of the mirror and imagining the swelling, cheering crowds of hot babes. Years later, I wouldn't be surprised if she was still posing in front of the mirror, a little looser but still wearing spandex. Madonna, a Leo, wore her spandex better than most, and Mae West, another Leo, would have worn spandex well had it been invented in her time.

Leo dykes can be agents of great political change as long as they are the out-front spokeswomen and not the worker bees in the back room, stuffing envelopes and answering phones. Frankly, we should leave that kind of work to the Virgos. Leos also have tremendous aptitude to sniff out change and opportunity, just like the lion sniffing out her prey. That may explain how a relatively obscure Austrian bodybuilder, Arnold Schwarzenegger (yes, a Leo) became a king of Hollywood.

moneY

Sapphic Leos are among the most generous souls in the zodiac. They like to use money to impress others and are therefore always willing to pick up the tab. And the grander the gesture the better, so if she invites you to dinner, don't hesitate to choose a wonderful and expensive place. Remember, you are only trying to make her feel better about herself!

She has an uncanny knack to make money, probably because she gravitates to high-profile careers like acting, which, if you are bold, pushy, confident and talented enough, can earn you the big bucks with relative ease. (Hey, it's not like working in a coal mine, bud.) She is her best promoter and can often get even her meager and half-assed efforts recognized and rewarded. In the corporate food chain, her professional plate always seems to be heaped with dessert—and rightly so, she says! (Did I mention that she always likes to eat the cherry? I suppose that's for another section.)

The Leo Home

It's easy to spot a typical Leo home. For one thing, it's the biggest on the block and probably hogs the corner. Sapphic Lions *love* excess and the more excess the better. Their tastes run to the extravagant though not necessarily tasteful objets d'art; large, plush furniture (preferably in jungle prints—*grrrrrrrr)* and shaggy carpets in excessively bright colors (especially the red and yellow palette). Curious to know who purchased that hideously oversized phony zebra-skin couch with horns for armrests? Guess who?

Every castle has a throne and every lambda Lion's house has a special living room chair that commands attention. It may range from an execrable, overdone La-Z-Boy recliner to an overdone Louis XIV sitter of crushed red velvet. Sitting in her chair is a capital offense punishable by death, so don't even think about it, sister.

She probably has a state-of-the-art entertainment center—only the biggest and best, natch! But don't ask her how to turn on the videotape machine and play back a tape. Who has time for such trivial matters? We leave that to detail-obsessed Virgos. Leo gals will just hand you the instruction booklet, if they can find it.

Lesbian Lions love to entertain but are not terribly interested in the nuts and bolts of putting together the event. Rather than waste time planning, purchasing and sweating over a hot stove, they would rather take everyone out for the evening or hire the best (obviously) party planners to take care of things. This leaves more time to impress their galpals with their obvious taste and style. Ah, but leave it to a Sag sister to stink up the room with her salami-smelling belches.

They drive big impressive cars, but may also have a couple of motorcycles or a Jeep around for spur-of-the-moment fun. These sisters tend to prefer large open spaces that are near enough to a metropolitan center or small bustling town so that excitement is never far away. Space is important to a Leo, so if she's short of funds and cannot currently afford what she wants, she is clear-headed and focused enough to carefully save for her future dream house: Hey, she's out of the closet, so why rent or own one?

Love, sex and Relationships

Because sapphic Lions are fire signs, this girl enjoys a robust sexual appetite. It is a lucky lovergrrl who has this big cat in her tank because when she's hot, she's out to demonstrate that she is the numero uno stoker and poker. However, be prepared to be second-in-command for the duration of the relationship. I'm probably exaggerating, but Leo gals are positioned to be the quintessential pillow queens who expect to be serviced first. And if she's not in the mood, neither are you, babe.

It is for this reason that some astrologers say that a lesbian Leo can sometimes be insensitive to partners' needs. How can anyone be sick in bed when I'm hungry and need attention? I know you're working on a big project, but I need someone to go to the movies with. If her needs are not deferred to often enough, she may gravitate to companionship elsewhere. She is a star, after all, who always needs an adoring audience of at least one and usually more than one to attend to her every need.

She can fall prey to false flattery and can be known to waste considerable time, energy and effort on lovergrrls who may not have her best interests at heart. Fortunately, she is not completely naive and will (eventually) catch on to the scam but not before she may have given short shrift to other, more appropriate gals. If you want to keep this proud Lion in your cage, be sure to pile on the praise (deserved or not) and massage her chest and flank areas. Leo rules the heart so find the way to her heart and lavish it with love and praise. Playing her sidekick is a small price to pay for the years of wonderment and fun she can provide.

In many respects, sapphic Leos are hopeless romantics, always clinging to the hope that the woman of the moment will become the woman of forever. This is because Leo rules the fifth house of romance, creativity and children. With all this happy energy surrounding her, even if the affair runs out of steam, it will be a fun ride for all concerned. Oh, and by the way, she loves the idea of a household full of kids, but because of her independent streak she may not be the one who stays home to feed them lunch every day.

friends

An amazon Lion loves to travel with an entourage of groupies. She boasts a wide and expansive circle of galpals who hang on her every word and agree wholeheartedly with all of her opinions. She is not solitary and would be a pathetically sad sight sitting in her pajamas, sipping tea at home alone on a Saturday night. Rather than mope and hide, she would gather the troops and burst in on the hottest dyke site in town and buy everyone a round of drinks. Make mine a Screaming Orgasm!

She does not easily confide in compadres; self-assessment is not part of her personal lexicon. For this reason, her entourage may veer toward more shallow, less deeply personal friends, acquaintances and "business" relations. Deeper connections (and their exposed vulnerabilities) are reserved for partners and maybe one or two bosom buddies but usually no more. This does not mean that she is reserved and standoffish; quite the contrary. This outgoing vixen is often the lifeblood of the party. However, while many can (and do) admire her and enjoy her convivial company, few can truly plumb her depths. Too bad.

family and parents

As long as they are given the acceptance and respect they so rightly deserve, a Leo dyke will get along fairly well with family members. It will certainly help if she is the baby of the family and therefore has been doted on and spoiled for most of her younger years. She is very proud of who she is and what she has accomplished in her life. If family members do not choose to recognize that or, worse, criticize her, she will find her own cheering section and go her own way. To hell with them. Good thing too, sister; no one should be expected to put up with a lack of respect or even homophobia from anyone, anywhere, at any time. Got that?

However, any emotional hemorrhaging within the family may take its physical toll on her. It is preferable and advisable to sit down together and hash out any problems. She has a tendency to internalize and that is not a good thing. Not only does it stress her heart, but it gives her a pathetic pall. I happen to cry at the sight of a sad Lion.

As a young cub, she was very active and popular, running for class president (and easily winning) or launching the school's most successful cookie drive. In later formative years, she might have pushed for campus reform and lesbian rights, including domestic-partner living accommodations and access to health care. She can make an impact on anything (or anyone) she chooses to. There are no barriers (or dams) she cannot overcome and that includes you, babe.

communication style

Feel a blast of hot air? Thar she blows! Sapphic Lions are the braggarts of the zodiac who tend to speak in hyperbole spiced with egoism. Whatever they think is correct *is* correct. Whatever they have is bigger and better than everyone elses. Some may find this attitude overbearing, but Leo babes chalk it up to mere jealousy.

Sapphic Lions are particularly adept public speakers because they think quickly on their feet, are eloquent and magnanimous, can read the pulse of the audience and play to the crowd. You just can't help but like them and their warm, inclusive humor. Bill Clinton (yes, a Leo) is a perfect example of this schmooze-ability. They always say just the right thing at just the right time, unlike mouthy Sagittarians who simply can't help tripping themselves up.

However, our Leo lass is not particularly good at accepting criticism (deserved or not), so try to couch your constructive remarks with a few compliments and make her think her behavior change was her great idea. On the other hand, she will always volunteer to cheerfully tell you what is wrong with you, your job, your appearance or your general life direction. Hey, really, no thanks is necessary; I just wanted to help.

At the same time she is a sucker for flattery and may become one of those women who dole out the last remains of their life's largess just to keep the empty compliments flowing. In later life, you can find her bolstered on her wobbly legs by a piece of buxom arm candy. Ain't true love grand?

health and fitness

Vanity will compel this girl to maintain her body (which is, after all, a temple to be worshiped) throughout her life. Taken to extremes, she can be found posing like Hulk Hogan (obviously a Leo) but with better plumbing. . . . She generally enjoys good health, bolstered and strengthened by an optimistic outlook, for most of her life. Depending upon other aspects of her astrological chart, a sapphic Leo can be prone to heart-related illnesses and should monitor herself for extra stress every so often. Even emotional turmoil can take its toll on this susceptible organ so keep your sunny side up, girlfriend, and don't fry it.

Leo is active and sporty, but don't expect her to run after your tennis balls. Remember: Captains of the team do not fetch. However, she can always be persuaded to tag team, especially in a tongue twister competition or a wrestling match. Pass the body oil, Marge!

Nothing is impossible for this irrepressible lass. Want to climb Mount Everest? She'll lead the way. Want to qualify for the Olympics? Stand aside and see how an expert does the high jump. Caution is advisable but not always followed. For this reason, she may also risk injury as her reach exceeds her grasp. Occasionally she is able to laugh off her failures. Occasionally.

shhh—secrets and fears

What's going on in the closets of a sapphic Lion? The areas of her solar chart that contain feelings of guilt, repression, ancestral baggage or family pressure are ruled by sensitive water signs. This means that, despite all outward appearances of robust independence, the Leo woman needs an inordinate amount of understanding and tender loving care for her to attain her fully affirmed potential. Sexually, she is a quivering feather waiting to be stroked. Spiritually, she is apt to be a hopelessly naive and romantic dreamer, yearning for some strong woman to carry her off and own her. When it comes to her family, rather than file any homophobic opinions under *G* for garbage, she secretly aches to be fully accepted for who she is and may spend an obscene amount of time, energy and effort to earn their respect and acceptance. Sometimes it's sadly in vain. But she will never admit to these secret vulnerable soft spots! Outwardly, she is an independent trendsetter who always commands respect and authority. Yeah, right.

weaknesses: are there any?

How could the proud Lion have a chink in her armor? Well, we've all got weaknesses. Aside from being insufferably pompous and arrogant, Leo dykes possess the uncanny ability to grab credit for everything and anything they do, including breathing. (Hey, but who does it better, babe?) They sulk if they are not the absolute center of attention, which may be cute in the early stages of a relationship but can quickly get old and tiresome. Want to drive them crazy? Tell them to pipe down or ignore them completely.

She is big on giving orders but not so great on taking them. Real problems arise when her vision is blurred by false flattery and vanity. Decisions made at this time tend to be mistakes . . . for all involved. But try to get her to admit the entire fiasco was her idea, or that it was even a fiasco. Ha! Forgetaboutit, baby!

She likes to be the grand dame of entertaining, but once the adoring crowd goes home she will not even attempt to help you clear the table or wash the dishes. Vacuum? That's your job, mama! And while you're up, can you get me a cup of coffee? On second thought, make it an espresso.

and in conclusion

The lambda Leo lass is a sight to behold: she is magnificent and resplendent and full of confidence and a sense of adventure. Tell her that she is number one and watch her bloom. Give her every-thing you've got and she will return the favor tenfold. Life would be dreary dull without her.

Madonna - August 16

who can ignore the royal charms of madonna, the regal lion? not many. proud, dramatic and not ashamed to strut her stuff, this gal, like all self-respecting lions, has to be the center of attention or there ain't no show. everything is out on the table for display from her many lovers (reputed, but not confirmed to be both male and female) to her personal hygiene. she is extremely aware of her persona and the way she presents herself to others. this is a woman who will always strive to be worshiped and admired. hey, sounds good to me. . . .

---

relationships with other signs

Did you meet the love of your life? Always examine her entire birth chart. In the meantime though, take a peek at these crass generalizations about sun sign compatibilities.

Leo and Aries—The fiery Leo-Aries combination is one of the best in both business and love. Each one respects the other's inde-pendence and personal successes, but there is also a mutual ad-miration society between them and they support each other and find ways of . . . ahem . . . vigorously celebrating together. Did someone mention wild and steamy sex? Yes, please!!

Leo and Taurus—When these two girlfriends plan a merger, it needs to be planned carefully. Proud Bulls will support any vi-sionary project the inventive Leo can conjure up, and the sapphic Lion can bank on the slow and steady progress of her bullish business partner. In love, the self-promoting Lion may soon tire of her couch potato lovergrrl. What a shame. Leo dykes may learn too late that one slow and steady hand is better than a theaterful of applause.

Leo and Gemini—These two independent sisters combine to make a worthwhile business partnership. Much can be accomplished by the blending of the energy of the expansive Lion and the inventive Twin. In love, a Gemini sister may tire of Leo's desire to be the grand dame and the lambda Lion may not cotton to the Twin's fickle, flirtatious appetite. Maybe Leo should change the menu every so often to keep "mind game Mary" second-guessing.

Leo and Cancer—Put these two gals to work. In business, the regal Lion lass likes to go forth and conquer new territory while her lambda Crab partner prefers to tend to the more mundane tasks and assorted gal Fridays. In a love relationship, the sapphic Crab would be expected to defer to the proud Lion in just about everything. *Grrrr,* that works for me, babe!

Leo and Leo—Did you ever, in a moment of fashion weakness, wear hot-pink paisley pants with a yellow-and-black-checked shirt? That competitive combination will give you a good idea of how a Leo-Leo relationship would play out. In business, both women want to be boss. Answer the phone? File? Forgetaboutit! In love, both demand fealty. My suggestion: Buy a pet instead.

Leo and Virgo—Don't discount the potential of a business relationship between a mighty Aphrodite Lion and a Virgin Venus. Expansive, fiery Leo sees the horizon and goes for the prize while the sensible Virgo reins in her partner's far-flung enterprises, giving it practical application. In love, however, there would have to be compromises. Virgo dykes don't like to take orders *all* the time and may find ways of lassoing the perky cat to keep her under control.

Leo and Libra—These two inspiring souls play off each other well. In business, they both offer considerable vision and creative solutions. (But find a Virgo to file for you.) In love, each one seems to instinctively know what the other needs from a back scratch to a warm shoulder. Great sex goes without saying.

Leo and Scorpio—The gregarious proud Lion has a burning innate enthusiasm that may be squelched by watery Scorp who will take credit for all the successes and distance herself from the failures. In love, the proud feline may not get the adulation she needs from her partner but will certainly get her fair share of sex. Ha! Who wants to be loved for her mind anyway!

Leo and Sagittarius—These two fiery mamas sure know how to have a good time together. Work seems like play, which means that relatively little gets done. In love, each one feels like an equal partner and doesn't let her better half get the better of her. Although it's more platonic than passionate, the chances for long-term commitment are good.

Leo and Capricorn—These two gals make an excellent business partnership, as long as sapphic Capricorn exerts patience and good humor. Lesbian Leo wants to be in charge but will not pry into the nitty-gritty day-to-day empire that the lambda Capricorn commands. In love, Leo finds a way to buy just the right things to win a Goat's heart. Ah, but can she hold on to that expensive heart?

Leo and Aquarius—The Leo-Aquarian combination will have its points of contact and moments of drift. On the one hand, both sisters may be so fiercely independent that they may operate beyond the other's sphere of influence. On the other hand, there may be a wonderful meeting of the minds and a powerful, positive connection that can spur any enterprise forward. But who will grab credit for the success?

Leo and Pisces—Get on your knees, girlie! In love, each one wants to be worshiped for the goddess she is. In business, Leo wants all the credit and none of the actual work, while the sapphic Piscean strains to be focused and directed. In love, lambda Leos ache to be admired and spoiled, while rainbow Fish need considerable nurturing and romance. Will these two great ships ever dock in the same port?

famous Leos: one a Day

Woody Harrelson	actor	July 23
Linda Carter	actor	July 24
Midge Decter	activist	July 25
Dorothy Hamill	athlete	July 26
Pina Bausch	choreographer	July 27
Jacqueline Onassis	first lady	July 28
Marilyn Quayle	lawyer	July 29
Eleanor Smeal	feminist	July 30
Evonne Goolagong	athlete	July 31
Iris Love	archaeologist	August 1
Myrna Loy	actor	August 2
Anne Klein	designer	August 3
Mary Decker	athlete	August 4
Loni Anderson	actor	August 5
Lucille Ball	comedian	August 6
Mata Hari	spy	August 7
Deborah Norville	news anchor	August 8
Whitney Houston	singer	August 9
Rosanna Arquette	actor	August 10
Allegra Kent	dancer	August 11
George Hamilton	actor	August 12
Annie Oakley	sharpshooter	August 13
Danielle Steel	writer	August 14
Princess Anne	royal	August 15
Madonna	performer	August 16
Mae West	actor	August 17
Robert Redford	actor	August 18
Coco Chanel	designer	August 19
Jacqueline Susann	writer	August 20
Princess Margaret	royal	August 21
Dorothy Parker	writer	August 22

women born on the cusp

Those born between August 19 and August 25 tend to have a combination of both Leo and Virgo attributes.

These sisters are among the most productive of the zodiac because they possess the uncanny ability to pace themselves, recognizing their limits of endurance, which are considerable. They are indefatigable workers and logical thinkers, blending the best of feisty, energetic Leo with disciplined, clear-thinking Virgo. This lady makes a great teacher or mentor, demanding the best from her students and from herself. She is a stern taskmistress, demanding fealty (Leo) and precise (Virgo) work habits.

The Virgin-Lion *loves* to get her hands in the earth and has a green thumb in addition to a couple of lavender fingers. Strangely enough, it is said that these buxom babes love to wander around in the buff, however, I am sure that she at least wears gloves when she gardens.

The way I see it, if you want a rainbow,
you gotta put up with the rain.
—Dolly Parton

virgo

August 23–September 22
The Delicious Virgin

Vital Statistics

Element = Earth (stability, functionality, process oriented)

Mode = Mutable (goes with the flow, adapts to change)

Ruling planet = Mercury (the planet of communication, thoughts and talks)

Ruling House = sixth (the house of the day-to-day job, health, pets)

Ruling part of the Body = intestines

Birthstone = onyx (August) or sapphire (September)

Best Day = wednesday

Lucky Number = 6

Astral color = gold, black, midnight blue

Flower = gladioli

Tarot card = The Hermit VIIII (wisdom that is acquired over time, caution)

The wise ancient seers dubbed those born between approximately August 23 and September 22 Virgo the Virgin, the sixth sign of the zodiac.

Astraea was known as the Star Maiden of innocence and purity. She was the daughter of randy Zeus and Themis (a.k.a. Divine Justice) and was sent down to earth to tame humanity—not an easy task, especially during the Iron Age. Earth was a lousy place to be at that time, full of barbarity and greed. (Sound familiar?) Not even even-tempered Astraea could keep this motley crew under control and she eventually gave up and took her place in the heavens as the constellation Virgo. She was evidently a practical woman who knew how to cut her losses.

general personality and first impressions

What this means is that lesbian Virgos have a sense of truth, justice, propriety and common sense all mixed in with a certain optimism. Unlike her stubborn earth sign sister Taurus, the wise and astute sapphic Virgin seems to know when the odds are simply insurmountable and impractical and when to give up the game and move on to more potentially successful endeavors. No naive time-wasting fool this gal! She leaves faraway, unattainable dreams to hopelessly romantic Piscean lasses. Virgo babes have their feet planted firmly on the ground and their priorities labeled and catalogued.

Virgo dykes look like the stereotypical librarians of the zodiac with a clean, crisp, no-frills appearance that seems to cry out for a good spanking or at least a sneaky peek under that long skirt. But those severe looks are deceiving, girlfriend. Virgo women actually have an immense capacity for love and loving. You just have to be patient enough to get through the layers of repression and guilt to reach the pearl. Persistent lovergrrls will be rewarded with a rich and fulfilling life partner who not only loves you for who you are, warts and all, but who also dusts and does windows.

Virgo is practical and no-nonsense and that goes for her wardrobe as well as her demeanor. This woman needs pockets, lots of them. And she wears sensible shoes that have that well-worn look because she's had them since high school. Who else would dry-clean her underwear and stitch a neat front seam into her cargo pants to give them a "cleaner line"? Who else arranges her pantry so all labels face slightly to the left? (Hey, how else can you easily read the ingredients?)

While genetics play a role in appearance, generally speaking Virgo dykes favor a cleancut, conservative look. (I would be hard-pressed to imagine one of these women wearing bangles, bows, frills and chiffon, but who knows? She may have an inordinate amount of Pisces in her chart.) Natural fibers were made for this gal; no qiana or (gasp!) spandex. Her idea of fashion sometimes seems to have stopped in 1957, but thank goodness for the invention of dry-cleaning!

Unlike other mutable signs (Pisces, Gemini and especially Sagittarius), the Virgo woman accepts change as an obligation rather than a joyful adventure. On some level there is a fear of the unknown (after all, she is a conservative earth sign), but mainly it's because she will be the one who will eventually bring order from the chaos and bring cleanliness after the mess. With every grand party, there has to be someone left to sweep up the confetti and stack the coffee cups. If you want something done right . . .

Lambda Virgos are modest and unassuming babes who tend to underrate their abilities and content themselves with toiling quietly in the background. (Crass grandstanding is left to sapphic Leos.) Virgos are not ones to grab the credit or demand rewards for their efforts. Sadly, sometimes this plays to their disadvantage. Lazy hangers on (like certain Pisces or Gemini) seem to glide through life on an oily song, while serious Virgos sweat in the back office and nurse their dishpan hands. More often than not, their efforts are eventually noticed and amply rewarded, but not before years and years of holding up the ladder so others can climb have elapsed. Watch those fingers, girlfriend!

career and work

Because Virgo rules the sixth house of the day-to-day job, health issues and pets, sapphic Virgins are happiest in careers that enable them to deal with nitty-gritty details, whether it's in accounting or nursing. They are meticulous, independent workers who are detail oriented and very neat and clean. You couldn't ask for a better office manager or veterinarian or even assembly-line worker. These gals can handle the repetitive tasks better than most women. In a very strange way, it gives them a sense of accomplishment; it's measurable and quantifiable, after all.

They are particularly adept at taking things apart and putting them back together. For this reason, they make excellent mechanics and engineers. Ask one to tune your engine sometime; she'll make it purr. They are also rather keen on giving advice, requested or not. Chances are they would make excellent social workers or psychologists or even art or theater critics.

Ideally they will engage in a profession that provides them with a sense of service; they are, in fact, some of the most giving women of the zodiac. (Except when it comes to money and we'll get to that later.) A career in the healing professions (like a doctor, dentist or nurse), in the educational arena (such as a librarian or researcher), as a shopkeeper, involving sanitation and disinfection or even as a geeky computer programmer all suit Virgo rather well. Facts and figures (yours included) turn on these gals. Give 'em a bunch of numbers to compute and they practically squeal with delight.

These proud babes are not considered especially creative or imaginative, but so what? What they lack in creativity they amply make up for in due diligence, steady application and reliability. Who needs to deal with time-wasting mind games when there is serious work to be done? Hey, move your butt and get back to work, pal! But dogged application sometimes has its drawbacks; sapphic Virgins concentrate on the littlest details and not necessarily on the big picture. There are times when she can doggedly traipse off on the wrong track, following the tiny bread crumbs on the ground and not the landscape's expanse. The secret to her success will be when she can balance the tiny details with the big picture and master both.

Virgo dykes consider themselves to be part of the lumpen proletariat rather than the royalty (there is only one Leo, after all) or even the petty bourgoisie. Just how lumpen depends upon their current circumstance and perspective. Mother Teresa (yes, a Virgo) is a classic example of how giving and sacrificing a Virgo woman can ultimately be. More corporately inclined Virgo gals will fight, for example, for domestic-partner benefits within her firm and content herself with dropping a quarter in some skell's dirty paper cup on occasion to get that charitable feel-good rush.

She treats her subordinates as her little chicks, worrying about them and even rewarding them with practical little gifts when they go beyond the call of duty like working seven weekends in a row. "Thank you for the new pencils, Ms. Virgo. They are certainly very sharp." Despite any hardships, those that work for her tend to become lifelong loyalists because she is the kind of boss who will pitch in and work as hard, if not harder, than anybody else. She will fight for fair compensation for her staff and her selfless attitude and lack of ego make her the consummate teacher of good work habits.

money

Sapphic Virgos are considered somewhat careful with their money, er, make that thrifty . . . okay, they can be downright cheap! Earth signs in general are considered practical and conservative with their dough, but unlike generous Taurus and tactical Capricorn, lambda Virgos don't have the confidence to spread their wad around or take great risks with their seemingly small sack of loot. Always concerned about being a burden on others in their old age, they carefully collect their pennies throughout their lives so as to build themselves a soft cushion for their later years. Sometimes it's a couch and sometimes it's a throw pillow, but it's all theirs, so hands off!

It's not just chronic financial worry that has this gal fixated on the bottom line; she is a woman who actually enjoys monitoring her money on an ongoing basis. There is something about spending a Saturday night tallying up her assets that gets this gal's blood pumping. Donate your jar of assorted coins to the cause and bring her to ecstasy. If the fates are kind, she'll find a well-endowed benefactress to keep her content on many levels in her later years.

She is a woman who wants to get full value for her purchases so if you see her arguing at the refund counter, assume that it was a factory or store screw up. If the item fails to live up to its promise, she wants her money back now—in cash.

The virgo home

Sapphic Virgins' homes have that clean and functional feel to them. Everything must be in its place, tidy and neat. Your Virgin's home may be decorated in serene colors designed to soothe her frayed nerves. This girl is a perfectionist in everything she does. Woe betide the Sagittarian gal who leaves her dirty undies on the couch, or worse, the pillow; a messy Sag girl won't be allowed in the bathroom without permission. Just as you would expect, Virgo sisters are so detail oriented that they will notice the one area of a seemingly perfect room where the dustballs lurk or where the throw pillow is askew.

No matter what part of the country she lives in, an amazon Virgo gravitates to quiet, conservative and rather ordinary neighborhoods; it is highly unlikely that she would choose to live next to the local Hell's Angels clubhouse. Too noisy and raucous. If through sheer circumstance she found herself next door to folks who have no concept of civic pride, she will more likely than not "help" her neighbors clean their front yards and scrub their sidewalks and quietly complain about them behind closed doors. She loves pets and they will be the cleanest and most well behaved in the neighborhood.

Lambda Virgos are earth signs and, as such, your Virgo probably has a beautiful, neatly tended garden. If space is a premium or she lives in an apartment, don't be surprised to see several window boxes carefully attached to the windowsill where she can grow herbs and other essentials. As ruler of the sixth house of health, expect to see several air purifiers and humidifiers around the house. You may wonder if she ever cooks in her kitchen; it's that sparkling clean. She does, but she is the kind of cook who cleans as she goes. It takes a bit longer, but it's better than having things in disarray. She can provide good, healthy meals with smaller-size portions. (It's not a good idea to stuff your face . . . with food, my Taurus gal!)

Want to tick her off? Rummage through her drawers and touch her private stuff. Use it without permission and leave it in a messy pile on the floor. Get your fingerprints all over it. Don't admit to it. Criticize her taste. Thought beheading was outlawed? Think again, babe.

Love, sex and Relationships

I have always found it amusing (and somewhat arousing) that Virgos have been designated as the Virgins of the zodiac. Maybe it's because they can appear so formidable and serious that many a faint-hearted woman won't even try to break through that stiff veneer to plumb their depths. Fact is, sisters, these babes are vixens under the sheets if you ever want to give them a taste. They simply don't believe in advertising all their merchandise to the general public. Good thing too; no sense in getting shopworn from too much rough handling.

Uncharitable astrologers sometimes say that Virgos are frigid. That is blatantly untrue! The fact is that she is fussy and discerning. She will patiently wait for the right lovergrrl to unclog her fountainhead but, in the interest of experience and comparison shopping, will go through a slew of ill-equipped plumbers in the meantime—and she doesn't mind letting them know when they fall short. Hey, I thought honesty was a virtue.

When Ms. Right does come along, stand back or be singed by the fireworks! The lesbian Virgin possesses great emotional depth and a sizzling sensuality that can satisfy any voracious appetite. (Three cheers for those lusty earth signs!) And she is loyal; once she commits, she's in it for the long term. Don't be surprised if, after the second date, she pulls up to your front door with a U-Haul containing all her worldly possessions (all labeled in neatly sealed boxes, no doubt). Just imagine all those years to come with a cleanly scrubbed bathtub! (You'll appreciate it after all those scented-oil bubble baths, my dear. . . .)

Don't expect her to drop everything and run off to Paris with you on the spur of the moment. She has too many commitments—both professional and personal—and too much of a sense of responsibility to simply drop everything midway and relax. At the same time, you can always rely on her to keep her commitments to you no matter how onerous or distasteful they seem to her. If she said she would go with you to your second cousin's bar mitzvah in Cleveland, she'll keep her promise. So what if it's Super Bowl weekend or—sob—the last weekend to buy those color-coded kitchen towels and containers on sale? Relationships are one big compromise—sniff!

friends

Unlike flirty Geminis, Virgo dykes are not "users" of people and don't tend to gravitate to the shallow glitterati and large anonymous party crowds. Despite being ruled by mindful Mercury, she is more of a thinker and an adviser rather than a schmoozer or mixer. She strives for intellectual compatibility and prefers to get beyond the superficial to one's inner core. She strives to get to know others well and see what makes them tick. This sapphic woman probably has a short list of bosom buddies with whom she spends a great amount of her personal time.

She can easily make friends from all walks of life but prefers serious "workers" rather than hopelessly dreaming "slackers." However, she is always there to help a friend through a bad patch, to a point, no matter how lazy they may be. There will be a time, however, when the well of compassion will dry up. It tends to happen when she perceives that her generosity is being taken advantage of and her kind efforts are not producing any substantive behavioral changes. After that point is reached, the best you can hope for is some terse practical advice and neatly typed directions to the employment office.

family and parents

A sapphic Virgo feels a sense of responsibility and duty to her family no matter how tough her childhood was. She can be relied upon to take care of Mom and Dad in their frail old age, even if that means she has to move closer to them and clean their bed-pans herself. (Who would do it better anyway?) Hopefully this sacrifice is willingly and joyously done as a thank-you for a happy, supportive and affirmed adolescence, not as a painful obligation expected by a pair of ogres. Chances are she is practical enough to understand her entire family's foibles and accepts them as part and parcel of having a full and complex life.

Virgo dykes tend to be sickly and frail as girls, with many minor ailments and sniffles. Wise parents understood their need to be coddled and supported and gave them the attention and myriad medications that they needed to get back in circulation. Despite all the days when they were home sick with drippy runny noses, they managed through dogged application, hard work and borrowed notes to be good students.

Because of their delicate constitutions, these girls were unlikely candidates for rough-and-tumble sports. More than likely, they were the editors of their school papers or members of the chess or debate team. Anyway, grass stains are too difficult to remove from clothing.

communication style

Kvetch, kvetch, kvetch. Virgo dykes love to complain about just about everything. Maybe it's because, with staticy Mercury as their ruling planet, they have so much nervous mental energy that it has to be released in any way it can. Feeling like crap today? Don't look to a Virgo for a comforting, undeserved compliment. What you will get is advice on how to get those unflattering tobacco stains off your teeth and how to improve your breath.

Virgos also don't suffer fools gladly and don't tend to engage in light-hearted banter or idle chitchat. This may give them the appearance of having absolutely no sense of humor. In fact, because they are earth signs, these women have a rather easygoing sense of humor and can laugh heartily at a good joke *(Good* joke, Taurus, not a fart joke) with a knowing hee-hee rather than a rousing, snorting guffaw.

Virgo dykes are linguistic perfectionists. They choose their words carefully and think before they speak, unlike their mutable sister sign Sagittarius . . . Remember, good penmanship, grammar and spelling are our friends! Virgo tends to dislike arguments and knock-down, drag-out fights. Like other earth signs, she would rather wear you down slowly with a harp, harp, harp and a carp, carp, carp.

Health and fitness

Sapphic Virgins tend to be slim, well toned and generally healthy although not necessarily robust. Virgo rules the intestines, which means that these mamas are more than a little obsessed with food, digestion and, *ahem,* regularity. If she asks you over for a drink don't be surprised if you're served a wheatgerm cocktail with a side of prunes. Hey, sister, roughage is our friend.

She tends to be a bit of a hypochondriac and can spend hours examining herself for moles that change shape and color or checking for unusual bodily smells. This is a girl who can sniff a burning cigarette from across a room . . . or a stranger's perfume on your clothing. Be warned.

While she is less likely to grunt and sweat at the local gym, she is not totally sedentary. Lambda Virgins are the consummate golfers. Where else can a woman stroll pleasantly over quiet, manicured greens and clean her ball at every hole. It's a veritable paradise!

shhh—secrets and fears

What do you find when you pry open the astrological closets of a lesbian Virgo? The areas of her solar chart that contain feelings of guilt, repression, ancestral baggage or family pressure are ruled by reckless and fearless fire signs. This means that, despite all outward appearances of stodginess and restraint, the Virgo woman secretly aches to spread her wings and soar to the sun. In the quiet of the night, she'll finger those leathered and lacy magazine pinups, getting wet at the thought of dominating a threesome or moresome. A perceptive lovergrrl will recognize that she secretly needs a tremendous amount of encouragement and support to attain her fully affirmed potential. Sexually, she is a raging fireball but she would rather dance naked at work than admit that administering the whips, chains and spiked ball bearings turn her on. Once you've gotten beyond the superficial with her, slip her a full-body, crotchless fishnet and she will be yours forever!

These are also the parts of her life in which she feels most vulnerable. Carelessly prod them and expect emotional outbursts that erupt like a fiery volcano spewing gullies of hot lava and leaving a trail of ashen remains. Some signs, like Aries, get off on that sort of thing, but conservative Virgins would rather pierce their tongue than get out of control like that. Ooooo, come to think of it, that may not be a bad idea.

weaknesses: are there any?

Even Lesbian Virgos have room for improvement.

Aside from being harping perfectionists, Virgo dykes can be hypercritical, going on and on like a broken record about things that are either still open to personal opinion and choice or are impossible to change. In extreme cases they can become overarching and preachy moralizers who seem to know better than anyone what's good for everyone. I would bet that Prohibition was conceived of by a Virgo.

There is also the risk that her perfectionism will goad her into taking on much more work than she can possibly handle effectively, thus dissipating her resources and taxing her health. Other savvier gals (no names, please, Leo or Gemini) can take advantage of this foible and play the lounging grasshopper to her industrious ant.

She must be careful not to be known as the girl with the ten thousand complaints who ruminates on her lovergrrl's tobacco-stained fingernails and cigarette breath. Somewhere along the way, she'll be relegated to the B list of party girls who are only invited when there are more than ten guests.

And in conclusion

Despite her fixations, sapphic Virgos are ready to support you in almost any inane thing you can think of to do. They'll be there for you, through thick and thin, making sandwiches, pouring the lemonade and cleaning up your mess. Their kindness, loyalty and earthy sexual appetite knows no bounds.

Relationships with other signs

While it is necessary to examine the entire horoscope in any relationship, it is possible to make some crass generalizations about sun sign compatibilities. Read ahead, girlfriend, but take it all with a grain of salt.

Virgo and Aries—Aries dykes wreck the landscape while Virgo mamas hold down the fort. In business, sapphic Rams make molehills out of mountains while lesbian Virgins expertly sweep up the dust. Will long-suffering Virgo eventually tire of cleanup

---

Lily Tomlin-September 1

Timing is everything with a perfectionist lesbian virgo, and Lily Tomlin is one woman who has carefully crafted her career all the way up the ladder. Lily is a rather private person and has been described as self-effacing. This virgo sister is not a headline seeker (. . . unlike some flashy geminis we know). Her projects are chosen carefully and methodically and must have a good purpose in the grand scheme. It's interesting that, for a comedian, she has a rather conservative and well-appointed appearance. No smelly sweatshirt and stained shorts for this gal in the public eye, unless, of course, it's a costume. And, like a true sapphic virgo, she prefers a long-term relationship. Just ask her partner. . . .

---

detail? Same situation in love: Aries women want a perennially hot patoot while queer Virgos are content with a hot toddy and flannels. Who will cool down first?

Virgo and Taurus—Practical Virgos are a perfect match for earthy Bulls for whatever life has to offer. These two bottom-line babes can make any business enterprise run smoothly and efficiently but may need to hire a visionary Gemini to cultivate expansion opportunities. In love, a romantic Taurus can sweep the stern Virgin off her feet. There is no telling where these two randy babes can wind up. At least I won't tell. . . .

Virgo and Gemini—Both of these women are ruled by expressive Mercury, so at the very least there will be a meeting of the minds when Virgo and Gemini dykes pair up. In business, Virgo keeps a watchful eye on the process while Gemini goes out and creates new opportunities. In love, the ever faithful Virgin may have to keep an ever watchful eye on her dallying partner while the fickle Twin gives her lovergrrl something to complain about.

Virgo and Cancer—Here is another meeting of the minds. The Virgo-Cancer combination is unbeatable in both business and love. Water nourishes the earth and helps things grow. One creates change while the other expertly manages it. Both women recognize the importance of sharing, commitment and working toward a common goal. They even complain in stereo.

Virgo and Leo—A business relationship between a lambda Virgin and an amazon Lion has great potential for success. The practical, earthy qualities of Virgo help maintain direction and the expansive, fiery touches of Leo spur the enterprise forward. In love, however, there would have to be compromises. Virgo dykes will not be bullied and may find ways of slipping saltpeter into the lusty lambda Lion's tea. Meow!

Virgo and Virgo—When these two school marms get together no one can get a complaining word in edgewise. Both have an overarching need to help and serve, which sounds great in principle but in reality is tiring. In love, they will either have a delicious lusty go at each other or be put off by each other's body odors. I give it a week.

Virgo and Libra—The practical Virgo dyke sees the languid sapphic Libra as too much of a pushover to be trusted in business. Heck, she'll give away the store just to be liked! In love, they're like two ships passing in the night; different interests, different social circles. If these two happen to meet up, I doubt whether there will be enough mutual interests to keep the fires burning. However, I could be wrong.

Virgo and Scorpio—The Virgo-Scorpio combination has a lot of potential both in business and in love. The earthy practicality of Virgo fits in nicely with the contemplative, strategic ability of Scorpio. In love, these two gals bring out the best in each other with sapphic Scorp unleashing the hidden Virgo vixen. Well, actually, sometimes she likes to be leashed.

Virgo and Sagittarius—The practical Virgo manner squares off with the seemingly haphazard momentum of the Archer. In business, the lesbian Virgin wants everything in its place while the sapphic Sag enjoys turning things topsy-turvy. In love, one is looking for a love match while the other just wants to lob the ball around. Virgins think Archers are out of control. Sags think Virgos are tight asses. You tell me.

Virgo and Capricorn—Here is a beautiful meeting of both mind and body. These two earthy babes are made for each other. In business, each understands the other's foibles and strengths. In love, the action never stops. Well, occasionally one has to take a break and earn a living between their three-course meals.

Virgo and Aquarius—The Virgo-Aquarian combination has its ups and downs. In business, the quiet application of lambda Virgo plays out well for the optimistic and expansive Aquarian dyke. In love, however, lesbian Virgins are too cloying, inquisitive and needy for the cold-blooded, independent Aqueerian. Alas, there could be lots of lonely nights when one is home sipping tea in front of the TV while the other is out painting the town lavender.

Virgo and Pisces—These two women have the potential for great success as either business partners or lovers. Each brings a new perspective that adds to rather than detracts from the party. Romantic, optimistic Piscean dykes can make the sapphic Virgo out to be a love goddess. It's nice to know that someone can do that!

famous virgos: one a day

Barbara Eden	actor	August 23
Cal Ripken Jr.	athlete	August 24
Althea Gibson	athlete	August 25
Geraldine Ferraro	politician	August 26
Mother Teresa	activist, nun	August 27
Ingrid Bergman	actor	August 28
Mark Morris	choreographer	August 29
Elizabeth Ashley	feminist	August 30
Caligula	emperor	August 31
Lily Tomlin	comedian, actor	September 1
Christa McAuliffe	astronaut	September 2
Valerie Perrine	actor	September 3
Mitzi Gaynor	singer	September 4
Raquel Welch	actor	September 5
Joseph P. Kennedy	businessman	September 6
Elizabeth I	royal	September 7
Patsy Cline	singer	September 8
Leo Tolstoy	writer	September 9
Amy Irving	actor	September 10
Kristy McNichol	actor	September 11
Jesse Owens	athlete	September 12
Claudette Colbert	actor	September 13
Kate Millett	feminist	September 14
Agatha Christie	writer	September 15
Lauren Bacall	actor	September 16
Anne Bancroft	actor	September 17
Greta Garbo	actor	September 18
Twiggy	model	September 19
Sophia Loren	actor	September 20
Stephen King	writer	September 21
Joan Jett	singer	September 22

women вoлn on the cusp

Those born between September 19 and September 25 tend to have a combination of both Virgo and Libra attributes.

This woman not only creates change but adapts quickly to every possible outcome. She has a combination of Libra's impulsiveness and joie de vivre and Virgo's desire to do good and make a difference in the world, though she is not as practical as one might otherwise expect. She loves animals and may have a houseful of strays that she overfeeds and indulges. Expect to find this gal in the country where she can tend a large garden and surround herself with nature in all its beauty.

This kind, graceful and unselfish babe is an enthusiastic lover-grrl, knowing just what to do to get a woman's juices flowing. Hopefully she will be able to find a partner who can match her attentiveness and generosity. If not, she is ready to make the best of a bad situation, falling back on her Virgo tendencies to go the distance even when the odds are stacked against her . . . up to a point. Ultimately, her Libra tendencies will encourage her to seek warmer climes.

*Tact is the art of convincing people
that they know more than you do.*
—Raymond Mortimer

✳

Libra
September 23–October 23
Balanced Fems

Vital Statistics

Element = Air (intellectual, conceptually oriented)

Mode = cardinal (conceives of and creates change)

Ruling planet = venus (the planet of beauty, love and art)

Ruling House = seventh (the house of marriage, any one-to-one relationships, open enemies)

Ruling part of the Body = kidneys

Birthstone = sapphire (september) or opal (october)

Best Day = Friday

Lucky Number = 7

Astral color = Black, crimson, light blue

Flower = Morning glory

Tarot card = Justice XI (balance, all-seeing, getting what one deserves)

☾

The wise ancient seers dubbed those born between approximately September 23 and October 23 Libra the Scales, the seventh sign of the zodiac.

Bacchus (whose Latin name is Liber—like Libra—get it?) is the god of wine, woman and song. No doubt a deity after my own heart. Bacchus was the son of the god, Jove, and the mortal, Semele. Juno, Jove's wife, was more than a little peeved at this infidelity and concocted a scheme to reduce Semele to a pile of ash. This she accomplished easily because, in general, mortals are stupid and gullible. Jove gave the infant Bacchus to the nymphs to raise. (Nymphs, eh? Some folks have all the luck!) Along the way, he learned the art of winemaking, and the rest, as they say, is history and hangover. Bacchus is regaled as not only the bearer of good, debauched times but also as a promoter of civilization and peace. Libra's ruling planet is Venus, the goddess of grace, charm, love and beauty, the half-sister of Bacchus and the mother of passionate Eros. Early worshipers built triangle-shaped temples for Venus. That's because the triangle symbolizes everything female. Talk about proud woman power!

General personality and first impressions

Because Venus is Libra's ruling planet, Libra gals are blessed with what I like to call the "hubba hubba" factor. They tend to be extraordinarily attractive, graceful and charismatic. They also know how to have a good time and can make everyone, no matter what their station in life, feel comfortable and at ease.

You can always spot a lambda Libra by peeking into the center of an adoring crowd. She's the one with the great smile and beautiful laugh who seems to hold everyone's attention. This gal makes an excellent first impression because everything she wears seems to look good on her, even a burlap sack. Lesbian

Libras tend toward the fem look, favoring clothing, accessories and selected pieces of jewelry that accentuate her coloring and grand style. Many of them are stunners both inside and proudly out.

It is no surprise that Libra is represented by the Scales (of justice). This is a woman who strives for balance in her life and equality for all. She is perhaps the most diplomatic sister in town, always finding a kind word or positive spin on even the most appalling situation. She also possesses infinite patience and the ability to put up with otherwise unbearable behavior from others. But she is no idiot. She is quite aware, thank you very much, that a particular someone is an asshole but feels that it would serve no good purpose to point it out to them. It would create unhappiness and imbalance. Unlike mouthy Sagittarius, blunt, no-holds-barred, unexpurgated honesty is not her strong suit. She would rather finesse than stink-bomb. However, don't peg her as a pushover, cousin; when diplomacy and tact fail, she will be one of the most fearless and fierce female fighters you'll ever see. She will do anything to restore parity and balance—even if it takes deadly force to do so.

But don't think that she usually flies off the handle; she is a tolerant woman and is not indiscriminate in her extreme reactions. In fact, she may often be accused of being unable to make final decisions. All air signs (Libra, Gemini and Aquarius) have a tendency to weigh all sides of an issue resulting in prolonged inaction while all the data is being processed. True justice grinds slowly, but remember that it also grinds exceedingly fine.

In afflicted charts she can veer to the extremes and should avoid overindulgence in (almost) everything. Tipping her scales too much to one side can make her excessively lazy and slothful. Tipping them too much to the other side can make her fanatical. Peace or war, take your pick.

career and work

Because Libra rules the seventh house of partnerships and relationships with a significant other, lambda Libras are happiest in careers that offer them opportunities to work with others on a daily basis. They need social interaction and a constant flow of ideas in their workplace to keep them stimulated and involved. There is nothing sadder than a Libra woman cooped up alone in a tiny airless office with no one to talk to or bounce ideas off of. If through afflicted circumstances she must take a job like that, expect to see her constantly surfing the Internet and haunting lesbian chatrooms for someone to connect with.

Lambda Libras have their finger on the button, so to speak, of what makes people tick. She seems to have an innate sense of perspective and balance that enables her to bring warring parties to the table of compromise. For this reason, she makes an excellent diplomat or mediator. Her sense of justice is acute. Expect to see her as a judge, lawyer, legal counselor or even political rebel fighting to achieve parity for the downtrodden. She may be across the negotiating table, arguing for women's rights, abortion on demand and domestic-partnership benefits. Like Libra Eleanor Roosevelt, one can achieve massive change with a diplomatic velvet glove wrapped around an iron fist.

With lovely, artistic Venus as their ruling planet, lesbian Libras can also succeed in any creative profession such as interior design, advertising, art, art consultation, cosmetology, music or even film. Their ability to make a silk purse out of a mangy sow's ear and a showplace out of a drab cubicle can lead them to a very successful career as a decorator or set designer.

money

Lambda Libras have a rather easy attitude toward money and finances. That is, easy come, easy go. They always manage to carry just a little less cash than what is required to cover the check. While this is not consciously intentional, their lack of fiscal planning can drive other, more practical gals, absolutely crazy.

At the same time, a Libra galpal can also be one of the most generous women you'll ever meet. She is not particularly materialistic and tends to acquire lovely objects more to beautify and harmonize her surroundings rather than to impress or empower. What hers is yours and vice versa. She has no compunction about going through your stuff and borrowing whatever catches her roving eye. Say good-bye to it, sister! She'll soon forget that it ever belonged to you and will happily lend it out to uhhhh . . . someone. . . . I forget who. Oh, did you want it back?

Despite this total disregard for fiscal prudence and healthy capitalistic acquisition, she manages through her life to either find a benevolent and generous sugarmama to take care of her needs or some other gushing monetary pipeline. Those that don't can be found hanging around the local dyke spot to scrounge up a free meal or just a happy-hour drink.

The Libra Home

Trying to locate a typical Libra's home? It's easy: It's the brightly painted one (with blended and coordinated colors à la Martha Stewart) with a front yard full of flowers and neatly tended shrubs. It is a well-designed showplace inside and out that demonstrates her impeccable taste in decor. She can make a cave warm and inviting.

Generally speaking, a lesbian Libra's home is well designed, neatly composed and well lit with comfortable, tasteful pieces of furniture and a nicely appointed entertainment area. She loves to have galpals over; the more the merrier! Like her sister air signs (Gemini and Aquarius), the Libra woman may move fairly often in her lifetime. She certainly tries to taste all the good things in life but, because of her lack of fiscal sense, she may have trouble meeting the rent or maintaining her general upkeep.

She is a great lover of animals (again, the more the merrier) and probably has a pack of dogs and cats roaming through the house. She has a heart as big as Texas and has to find a home for every stray she finds. Don't be surprised if one or two of them share her bed.

love, sex and relationships

This gal is a babe magnet. Blessed with innate charm and sex appeal, her only concern is choosing who among the favored few to bestow her favors upon. She is often swayed by a pretty face and great bod (but, hey, who wouldn't be?) and has a rather large sweet tooth for decadent desserts (no names, please). As with other air signs (Gemini and Aquarius), she is a flexible lover. This means that not only is she somewhat of an accomplished acrobat, she is also rather experimental. Her list of lovergrrls spans a wide range of personality and body types. Threesomes are not unusual, nor is an occasional man (chalk that one up to a lack of taste and go on). What she lacks in spontaneity, she amply makes up for in delicious variety. Love is quite an adventure!

Generally speaking, while the sapphic Libra is ideally looking and hoping for a life partner and not some quick flick and lick, she is prone to infidelity. The idea of growing old alone and relying on the kindness of strangers is anathema to her. However, because she is incredibly idealistic in love, many seemingly small things can scuttle the love boat and set her mind wandering. For long-term happiness she must be careful in choosing her lovergrrls, valuing practical compatibility rather than hot spurts.

Interested in snagging and shagging this gorgeous creature?

Her Q spot is in her mind so send her charming little love notes that spark her imagination and fuel her vanity. Then wisk her off to some beautiful locale and wine and dine her. When you get to know her a little better, share everything with her, especially your deepest, darkest secrets. Unlike maniacal Scorpio, a sapphic Libra will never hold them against you (unless you beg her to) and may even take the hurt and sting out of them for you by giving you a new and clearer perspective.

friends
Because they are social beings, Libra lasses have trouble being alone and doing things without at least one bosom buddy to hang on to. The idea of going to a movie solo, eating dinner in a restaurant alone or taking a vacation for one is simply too painful and depressing to contemplate. For this reason, Libras tend to surround themselves with a bevy of attractive galpals and tend to travel in social packs. College was probably a happy time for them with its highly social dormitory life, cosy roommates and, of course, the gang showers.

Libra dykes are social butterflies who seem to know everybody and vice versa. More often than not, they are the epicenter of the party, surrounded by the most attractive babes in the room and carrying on delightful, witty conversations with all in their general vicinity.

If you want to spend time with her, don't ever keep her waiting. This is one woman who can't stand to cool her heels on a street corner or alone at a bar. You'll get fifteen minutes grace, maybe, before she makes other plans. You have been warned!

family and parents

This gal has a rather interesting relationship with her family. On the one hand, she can be very supportive of the whole motley crew and even tolerant of their assorted strange peccadilloes, going so far as to sublimate her true needs and desires to preserve family harmony. But tip those scales with too much of that garbage and watch out! She will tear apart those family ties with a frenzied zeal that can bring tears of joy to your eyes. Sensitive and caring parents will give this young girl the freedom to make her own affirming choices later in her life. They will be rewarded with a daughter who will be there for them through thick and thin.

Lesbian Libras tend to have been extremely popular girls in school. They were the ones who wore tight sweaters and short skirts and who cracked their gum rather seductively. Probe your Libra and you may find that she was a cheerleader in high school. The funny thing about these girls is that while they were considered popular and had many fleeting acquaintances they probably had just one or two very close confidants with whom they traded secrets and used gum.

This is a girl who could easily glide through school on others' hard work, turning on the charm if she needed to copy someone's homework or obtain test answers. Yet, strangely enough, she never seemed to get caught with her academic pants down. Maybe that's because she is inherently smart, albeit slothful.

communication style

Libra girlfriends are very talented orally. She is known for her diplomacy, savoir faire and general good manners and has the uncanny ability to say the right thing at the appropriate moment. This gal could give lessons to sister Sagittarius! Those who do not know her well may mistake this politeness as a sign of acquiescence, but don't be fooled! Libra dykes are some of the most stubborn and forceful babes when they are pushed. It should come as no surprise that some of the most decorated generals in modern warfare (such as Eisenhower), are, in fact, "diplomatic," "wishy washy" Libras. Let's just say that they can be flexible but don't try to bend them in half.

Health and fitness

Libras are associated with the kidneys, which, when you think about it, makes a lot of sense. The kidneys balance the bodily functions by cleaning out the impurities and optimizing one's healthful intake. For this reason, Libras tend to drink an inordinate amount of water to cleanse their bodies and flush their systems.

A Libra can be a bit on the lazy side and may find it hard to stay on a diet. Like her sister sign Taurus, her idea of strenuous exercise is lifting small amounts of chocolate from the box to her mouth. Try to find creative ways to satisfy her sweet tooth without the glucose. Think of her as a graceful marathon runner rather than a heated sprinter. She does her best in moderation— overindulgence of any kind (whether in food, drink or, *ahem*, strenuous exercise) is not advised. Slow and steady is always better in my book, girlfriend.

shhh—secrets and fears

Here is a nasty little closeted secret about lambda Libras: The areas of her solar chart that contain feelings of guilt, repression, ancestral baggage or family pressure are ruled by sedate earth signs. Outwardly, she happily nibbles at the sexual smorgasbord, sampling the fish, the oyster, the sweetmeat and the occasional foul. But those that know her well realize that she yearns for a stable and loyal soulmate who's in it for the long-term. Spiritually, she is much more conservative and risk-averse than she lets on. In fact, if left to her own deeply submerged devices, she can become automatic and inflexible in her beliefs. When it comes to her family, she might have felt that she didn't measure up to Mom and Dad's expectations and may unconsciously spend an inordinate amount of time seeking their approval. If this useless behavior should ever manifest itself, I would advise her to lie on the couch and probe her feelings.

weaknesses: Are There Any?
No one is perfect, babe.

Aside from being shallow, Libra sisters can be so laid back they can sleep through sex. Some may call them lazy, but astute astrologers know that they work rather hard at finding others to do the difficult and dirty work for them. They have the uncanny knack of dropping in for a visit around dinnertime, bringing nothing but a healthy appetite and their latest ravenous girlfriend. Forget about reciprocation; they never have enough money on them to pay for yesterday's stale bagel and rancid butter, much less a cheap dinner for you. Hey, just having them around should be enough!

What else? Some truly afflicted types hate to be seen around those whom they consider to be their physical inferiors. Only the most attractive need apply to this henhouse. It doesn't even matter if these goddesses have lousy personalities or all the spark of a wet turd. Looking fabulous wins the election in her nation.

And in conclusion
For pure charm, grace and beauty, stake your claim on a sapphic Libra. This popular kitten can make you feel like a tiger. She is

artistic and creative with the ability to turn any sorry sight into a sight to behold. Life with her will never be dull and, in fact, can be absolutely fabulous.

Eleanor Roosevelt - October 11

Eleanor Roosevelt probably best epitomizes the carefully balanced nature of a Libra. she was extremely diplomatic, but she was no pushover. A true humanitarian, she was able through her innate charm, diplomacy and grace, to accomplish great humanitarian feats. Not afraid to take a controversial stand, she was able to create bridges of understanding and cooperation. while I can't speak to her sexual proclivities or acrobatic prowess, her letters to her bosom buddy demonstrated a keenly romantic appetite . . . at least on paper!

Relationships with other signs

You need to look at a woman's entire chart to really determine compatibility. However, for a thumbnail sketch, read ahead.

Libra and Aries—Brash lesbian Rams have met their match in the smooth and graceful lambda Libra. In business, the amazon Aries boldly goes forth and conquers new territory while her delightful partner tames the beast within and keeps the office looking fabulous. In love, the sexy Libra lovergrrl keeps her Ram happily penned in. Somehow she knows exactly what this fiery babe needs to keep her energy up.

Libra and Taurus—Both Libra and Taurus are ruled by mighty Aphrodite, which means that despite their personality differences they manage to find some common ground. In business, the sociable Libra lady may sometimes feel restrained by her stolid partner but can keep plans moving ahead while Taurus solidifies and consolidates. In love, one gal's chateaubriand may be another's meat and potatoes. Share a bottle of wine and celebrate your differences!

Libra and Gemini—These two airy mamas will be attracted to each other from the get go. This relationship may be less successful from a business point of view as neither woman is particularly good at tackling the nuts and bolts or attending to the more mundane tasks. However, in love, these two are romantic, harmonious and happy campers. Leave the business decisions to your Capricorn accountant and work on making love.

Libra and Cancer—The breezy Libra manner may grate on the sensibilities of caring Cancer gals. In business, the Libra babe does lunch while the sapphic Crab manages the accounts and generally runs the office. In love, who parties all night with a bevy of bosom buddies and doesn't call home even once?

Libra and Leo—These two expressive gals form a happy and zesty combo. In business, they both offer considerable vision and creative solutions. (Find a down-to-earth Capricorn to plan and process for you.) In love, they can read each other's minds. Leo ladies want to be treated like royalty and lesbian Libras are the consummate diplomats. Before she knows it, the Lion will be purring at the feet of you know who.

Libra and Virgo—Lovely Libra lasses may be too lackadaisical for sensible Virgos who run tight ships both in business and in love. Libras are canoodling with clients while her partner hangs around the office percolating the coffee, collecting paper clips and keeping the office functioning seamlessly. In love, one woman's delicious passion is another's icky mess. Maybe you can convince her to pretend she's a tablecloth and lick her clean.

Libra and Libra—Two lesbian Libras make a jolly pair of book-ends indeed. They are both so even-tempered that any type of relationship should be relatively argument free. There is a balance achieved in the workplace where both seem to know what is expected of them and do their darndest to please each other. Their love life is, well, lovely. Jeez, Louise, how boring can two gals get?

Libra and Scorpio—The breezy gay Libra personality may be crushed by the intensity of lesbian Scorpio. In business, even her best efforts can be denigrated as frivolous and worthless by her more serious and tactical partner. Love relationships are all sex and little chitchat. Talking just wastes valuable time, says lusty sister Scorp. When she wants to plumb your depths, she's not talking philosophically.

Libra and Sagittarius—This enthusiastic pair spends most of their business hours going off on tangents. Both love to play rather than buckle down and work. Advice: Hire a Capricorn dyke to keep things on an even keel and balance the books. In love, air stokes fire, don't ya know. Try to stoke, stroke and poke as often as possible.

Libra and Capricorn—These two gals are well-balanced business partners: Lesbian Libras can rein in and direct depressive Capricorn dykes when the pressure becomes too great. One has enthusiasm but little practical application while the other can see trouble coming and amply prepare for it. But, ah, in love, Capricorn sisters can't help but take the romance out of an evening. How long will the achy-breaky energy last before lickety-split Libras look elsewhere? Where's my stopwatch?

Libra and Aquarius—The airy combination of Libra and Aquarius brings together two great minds in a zesty confluence. In business, these girlfriends are unbeatable for generating enthusiasm and great ideas. (They also test the limits of their expense accounts.) In love, they can stay up for hours just chin-wagging. Their tongues get a pretty good workout too.

Libra and Pisces—There is much to recommend a Libra-Pisces partnership, but at the same time tremendous patience will have to be exerted to keep this flagship from pulling out of port. In business, neither one is well equipped to make difficult decisions. In love, lesbian Fish find themselves holding down the fort while party-hearty sapphic Libras paint the town with a bevy of bodacious babes. My advice: Get a cat instead. They are more independent.

famous Libras: one a Day

Bruce Springsteen	singer, songwriter	September 23
Linda McCartney	photographer, musician	September 24
Barbara Walters	journalist	September 25
Olivia Newton-John	singer	September 26
Meat Loaf	singer	September 27
Brigitte Bardot	actor	September 28
Madeline Kahn	actor	September 29
Angie Dickinson	actor	September 30
Julie Andrews	singer	October 1
Annie Leibovitz	photographer	October 2
Emily Post	etiquette expert	October 3
Susan Sarandon	actor	October 4
Bob Geldof	musician	October 5
Carole Lombard	actor	October 6
Desmond Tutu	activist, clergyman	October 7
Sigourney Weaver	actor	October 8
John Lennon	singer, songwriter	October 9
Helen Hayes	actor	October 10
Eleanor Roosevelt	first lady, activist	October 11
Luciano Pavarotti	singer	October 12
Margaret Thatcher	politician, prime minister	October 13
Hannah Arendt	philosopher	October 14
Penny Marshall	director	October 15
Suzanne Somers	actor	October 16
Rita Hayworth	actor	October 17
Martina Navratilova	athlete	October 18
Patricia Ireland	activist, feminist	October 19
Bela Lugosi	actor	October 20
Carrie Fisher	actor	October 21
Sarah Bernhardt	actor	October 22
Gertrude Ederle	athlete	October 23

women born on the cusp

Those born between October 20 and October 26 tend to have a combination of both Libra and Scorpio attributes.

How do you balance and harmonize the easygoing attitudes of Libra with the passionate Sturm und Drang of Scorpio? It ain't easy, girlfriends, and the sister who straddles Libra and Scorpio will grapple with her ying and yang energies throughout her life.

The queer Scaly Scorp is a creative thinker, master strategist and as close to genius as one can possibly get without being insane. Ideas originate and germinate with intense frequency so you gotta be quick around her to catch all the gems. With the perseverance of Scorpio and the adaptability of Libra, this proud woman is both tenacious and a risk taker and can be successful in any and all undertakings. She makes a fairly astute general or political adviser.

The most delicious aspect of this cusp placement combines the beauty of Libra with the passion of Scorpio. Let's face it, these sexual stunners are goaded by their gonads and they feast at every meal. Happily, since they traverse both the seventh house (of partnerships) and the eighth house (of sex), they don't have to go far to satisfy their appetites. Dessert, anyone?

P

the greatest minds are capable of the greatest vices
as well as of the greatest virtues.
—Descartes

scorpio

October 24–November 22
The Girl with the Stunning Tail

Vital Statistics

element = water (fluidity, emotionally oriented)

mode = fixed (fights change, attempts stability)

Ruling planet = pluto (the planet of volcanic change and immense personal power)

Ruling House = eighth (the house of sex, sex and more sex, death, taxes, psychological breakthroughs)

Ruling part of the Body = genitals and anus

Birthstone = opal (october) or topaz (November)

Best Day = Tuesday

Lucky Number = 8

Astral color = Black, golden brown

flower = calendula or cosmos

Tarot card = Death XIII (transformation, new beginnings, phoenix rising from the ashes of the past)

The wise ancient seers dubbed those born between approximately October 24 and November 22 Scorpio the Scorpion, the eighth sign of the zodiac.

The intensely passionate sign of Scorpio is represented by a scorpion. Why? Scorpions are rather dangerous creatures with highly toxic tails that they are not above using from time to time. Ouch! They have a rather hard shell protecting a soft, highly vulnerable inner core. This shell is a protective armor and the highly poisonous tail is a protective weapon against the dangers of day-to-day life. With all this artillery poised and ready against the harsh outer world, there can sometimes be a slip up; her tail is so poisonous that if she accidentally stings herself instead of her enemy, it is a fatal mistake. Remember: The scorpion is the only animal that can kill itself. This hazard underscores the themes of death and regeneration associated with this highly toxic persona. The other animal associated with the sign of Scorpio is the eagle, which highlights the promising possibilities of the sign to soar above all others in a graceful, majestic display of selfless courage. However, most folks don't usually get to see those attributes . . .

General personality and first impressions

With all these severe and nasty underpinnings, it is no wonder that Scorpio women often get the worst rap in the zodiac. Uncharitable astrologers would say that these gals deserve every nasty thing written about them, but I really have to disagree. Sure, they are conniving, vicious and vengeful, but they are also a house on fire sexually and possess the greatest energy reserve this side of Three-Mile Island. Death, revenge, sex and taxes are not areas where a girl can easily straddle the fence. In fact, this calculating mama doesn't straddle the fence at all. She does, however, straddle where it has the greatest impact: over lovergrrls.

Did you happen to stink-bomb her locker in the second grade? She not only remembers it with clarity but is still nursing the insult and plotting her revenge—that is, if she hasn't already exacted it several times over. She is the scorekeeper of the zodiac and (as with sex) once is never enough! Think twice before you try to trip her up unless you want to know what a broken toe feels like.

Scorpios are often associated with blood and menstruation. The imagery is powerful: Menstruation is the breaking down of a potential life but offers the promise of future life-giving opportunities. Death and regeneration are not subjects for simpletons or those faint of heart. Maybe that's why these mamas tend to attract other intense types to pal around with. Who else would want to bring popcorn to a surgery theater? (No? I guess we can always eat after the vivisection.)

You can recognize a typical Scorpio sister by her passionate nature and serious appearance. Genetics always play a role, but she may be dark-featured with soulful yet piercing eyes that don't miss a trick. She dresses not only to impress but also to create a persona. If tatoos, overalls and jackboots are de rigueur, she's got to have 'em (and will wear them well). But if she's a corporate animal, expect some high-priced, high-style imported suits in her wardrobe. And money is no object either, cousin.

This woman is a complex soul caught in a world that strives for simple answers. For this reason she may experience bouts of depression or frustration. A wise lover or galpal will find creative ways to take her mind off such things. Gee, I wonder what will do the trick?

career and work
Because Scorpio rules the eighth house of sex, death, taxes and "other people's money," amazon Scorps are happiest in careers

that give them the opportunity to do meaningful, dramatic work. They are interested in getting to the bottom of things both figuratively and literally. In addition to being terrific investigators and psychiatrists, sapphic Scorps can become excellent gynecologists or proctologists. After all, Scorpio rules the genitals and anus. Perhaps this means that she is interested in assorted odds and ends.

This woman is a smooth operator with the ability to blend into the background or take charge at any time. Her preference, however, is to be the power behind the throne and for this reason tends to enter careers where she can play the puppeteer to some hapless marionette. She can be found in a variety of back-office, powerbroker positions such as adviser to a president (or despot) or in positions that require persistent investigative skills, such as a journalist, detective, doctor (especially a psychiatrist), policewoman, mechanic or inventor.

Blood and gore are no problem for this gutsy lady. Expect to see her engrossed in an autopsy trying to figure out the cause of death. (And don't be surprised if she does this on her lunch hour between bites.) Other, less-robust signs faint at the mere mention of carnage, but she tends to gravitate to it if only to find out what happened. She could be one of those United Nations workers traveling to the suffering parts of the world in an attempt to correct a bad situation.

It should be noted that these magnificent gals are considered to be the healers of the zodiac and possess great vibratory force, magnetic connection and remarkable skill in their hands. (Hey, sister, spend some of that talent on me!) These gals emit a healing influence on others that can calm turgid waters. A Scorp makes an excellent surgeon. She may appear unsympathetic and removed and have a miserable bedside manner, but she will come through in the clutch in the operating room with her self-control, clearheadedness and determination to find and eradicate disease from the system.

Altruistic women of this sign have great personal reserve and persistence to get to the root of a wrong and correct it. They make excellent lawyers because they are not easily rattled, don't mind trawling through miles of legal verbiage, have great memories for precedence and, like most sharks, are prepared to go for the jugular. Remember, kids: The more blood the better with this babe.

Her eloquence, tact and ability to influence can enable her to become a powerful public speaker, even developing a pulpit and flock of crazed followers. In full bloom, she can exert strong influence for political extremists. Let's not forget that both Leon Trotsky and Pat Buchanan fall under the sign of Scorpio.

This is a woman who doesn't mind working hard and putting in the hours to get a job done. Many of these mamas are workaholics who will hunker down to complete a particular project over the weekend. She is a formidable corporate competitor and usually has the smarts and the talent to go the distance up the food chain. Even as an entry-level lackey, she can demonstrate an aptitude for future advancement. Throw her some red meat and see how she chews it up.

money

The power of money and what (and who) it can buy is altogether intoxicating for this passionate gal. Old-time astrologers say that she is a supreme manipulator when it comes to money, but that is not altogether accurate. Actually, she is a supreme manipulator in other areas of her life too, particularly in love, but we'll get to that later.

The fact is, she is a brilliant financier and can amass considerable fortunes through her innate strategic and intuitive abilities. This is a woman who knows how to play the stock market and win, win, win. Whereas her sister sign Cancer can stockpile tiny amounts of money (mostly change) into a small fortune, Scorpio dykes work on far grander scales. This is the gal who moves millions and eventually buys out Donald Trump and makes him paint her house. (I knew a man was good for something.)

Some may say that she is conniving and selfish, but those naysaying women are just jealous Janes who secretly yearn to be bought and sold by this powerful Scorpio dyke.

The scorpio Home

Sapphic Scorpios are always cognizant of the impression that they make on others. The way they dress, the way they speak and even their home surroundings tend to be a reflection of this calculated "public persona." Everything from what neighborhood they choose to their furnishings and accoutrements will fit this "outer" face. Because of this, Scorp homes will vary according to taste and psychology. My imperfect sample runs the gamut from bowl-'em-over opulent and showy with fine art and antiques displayed in every room, even the bathroom (Be careful with those wet hands, girlfriend) to austere and almost garretlike with furniture from the Salvation Army and the street. Go figure with these mysterious gals!

One thing is constant: Their homes are clean and they have one or two hidden places where a girl can just be herself, whatever the hell that would be. Should you, on your way to hanging up your coat, stumble upon the "tie me up—tie me down" room, make a mental note of it for future reference and tell her that you just got lost.

If they fancy themselves audio fanatics, expect to see a state-of-the-art showroom in their living room. If they eschew these worldly items, a simple turntable or eight-track will do, thank you very much. If they fancy themselves consummate epicureans, their kitchen will be well stocked with the most beautiful cookware and obscure spices. But if they prefer to spend their waking hours feasting only on raw female, all you may be able to rustle up is a can of SpaghettiOs from the early 1980s and a bottle of water of undetermined vintage. My advice: Make reservations and avoid any possible nasty surprises.

love, sex and relationships

This girlfriend smokes and, believe me, where there is smoke there's a raging fire. Ouch! She possesses the innate water sign ability for deep probing intimacy and strong emotion and takes it one giant step further than sister water signs, Cancer and Pisces. Once is never enough for these sexually robust mamas and she is one of the few women who can bring out the best in anyone during lovemaking—even repressed Virgos and Capricorns. Want to feel like a woman liberated and soaring to the highest heights? Find yourself a passionate Scorpio lovergrrl and hop on.

But with every trip to the moon with gossamer wings, there is a price to pay and it's just one of those things: Sapphic Scorps are secretive and not altogether trustworthy. They are also among the most jealous and possessive women on the planet. Amazon Scorps tend to love on their own terms, requiring the utmost loyalty and fealty, but it's not always tit for tat. (She is always ready just to give tit, however.) She tends to be more interested in the consummation of relationships rather than the dreary day-to-day maintenance of them. For every night of whipped cream and chocolate sauce licking feasts, she tends to forget that there will be days of morning mouth and dirty, sticky hair.

The enlightened, mature Scorps of the species eventually learn that in order to maintain a healthy long-term relationship, they need to slowly stoke and poke the flames of passion day to day and night by night rather than burn the fire out quickly with a stint of different lovers. Otherwise they may find themselves in old age, lusting after perky young things who won't even rub their nipples against them while pushing their wheelchairs. A sad spectacle indeed!

More than a few S and M types come from the Scorpio camp. Don't be surprised if she asks you to play "slave" to her "master" during loveplay. If nipple clamps, zippered masks and leather straps are not your thing, search the zodiac for a solid earth sign (Taurus, Capricorn or Virgo) who won't truss you before she cooks and devours you. However, don't knock it if you haven't tried it.

A clever lover who can catch her eye and hold her attention will be rewarded with a life of intensity, sexual passion and excitement. Consider the fun you'll have in a lifetime role in *The Taming of the Shrewd.*

friends

Sapphic Scorpios tend to hang around with a small circle of trusted and trusting galpals. Some may call her group more of a cadre of secretive, cliquish outcasts, but that is not necessarily true. Sure, she is highly suspicious of the status quo and tends to gravitate to more . . . unusual types, but just because they all have tatoos on their scalps doesn't mean that they don't share a number of mainstream values.

The best part about having a Scorpio girlfriend is that you never have to worry about forgetting seminal events in your life. She will happily remind you about the time that you wet your pants in kindergarten on parent-teacher day or when you accidentally spit food at the boss at an important business lunch. You two will chuckle about it for years to come. . . . Then again maybe just she will.

Unless her chart is adversely afflicted, amazon Scorps tend to make friends for life. However, to know her is to never really know her. She is a woman with many layers, like an onion, and peeling them back can bring tears to the eyes. She does not willingly reveal secrets about her soul, and it may only be through a personal and painful period that you learn about things that made her who she is today. Even then you may never really know the whole, true story.

She can be very generous around those whom she trusts and can throw some of the most exciting parties in town. Expect to see one or two hotshots working the crowds along with assorted glitterati and poseurs. You'll find the hostess in the background making sure certain people are talking to other certain people or in the kitchen bossing the staff around. Love the caviar!

family and parents

Scorp dykes can have fairly good relationships with their parents, however, because they are so secretive, I wonder whether their parents truly know everything about them. Homophobic households were childhood prisons for these girls, but it is very possible that your Scorp took her revenge for such oppression years and years and years later, even if she totally cut her ties to the family. Something to think about, folks.

As a young student, she probably gravitated to behind-the-scenes powerbroker positions at school, such as editor of the school paper or director of the senior play. Positioning herself as the center of attention, such as running for class president, might not have been as palatable, although with her innate determination and persistence it would have been achievable. A simple byline would do nicely, thank you. Gee, I wonder who wrote those scathing "anonymous" letters to the editor?

Sapphic Scorpios are bright but intense girls who rarely let out a belly laugh or even a jolly snort for that matter. Don't expect her to be elected Miss Popularity or even Miss Congeniality (and what self-respecting Scorp even cares?), but she is a shoo-in for Most Likely to Succeed. Prom queen? Cheerleader? Forget-aboutit, sister!

Smart parents who could figure out what she was all about probably gave her all the intellectual stimulation and moral support she needed to feel happy and affirmed. These were the girls with the chemistry and Erector sets at a time when Barbie was being shoved down their throats. (However, there is something to be said about pairing Barbie with Midge.) Even as a kid she was a collector: books, bugs, you name it. Her room was a center of mystery, wonder and assorted crap.

communication style

Lesbian Scorps mean what they say and say what they mean, but only if you listen very carefully. She is the proverbial iron fist wrapped in a velvet glove. She is very self-possessed and controlled in her speech and can easily manipulate lesser minds to get anything or anyone she wants. While Gemini babes are flirtatious, Scorpio gals are persuasive, so be warned. Once she sets her sights on you, you have no chance to escape. One minute, you'll be hip to hip at the bar and the next minute hip to elbow at her place. At least then she can put her tongue to better use than inciting a revolution. Storm the barricades . . . or perhaps the vulva?

Her command of the language can naturally lead her into politics, preferably as a behind-the-scenes adviser.

Tell her your darkest deepest secrets without fear of broadcast . . . for the time being. If you ever piss her off, it will become fair fodder for the gossip mill and even the front page. Her own personal secrets are just that, babe—secret. So don't even try to get her to confide in you. Even things that you think she has inadvertently let slip in a moment of weakness are calculated press leaks designed to position herself and motivate others.

Health and fitness

Sapphic Scorps are virile gals who can withstand ongoing torture and even the occasional cold and flu. They tend to have strong constitutions, even if they are not particularly active or athletic. While other water signs (Pisces and Cancer) are generally thought of as less robust and prone to bouts of depression, nervous conditions and general nagging ailments, Scorpio dykes are about as frail as a driving steamroller or a falling anvil.

However, because Scorpio rules the genitals and anus, they must take care to protect these private parts from infection and ongoing stress. A constant diet of especially spicy foods and teeth-grinding anxiety could result in hemorrhoids, for example. Yeast infections are fairly common with these women as well. The secret is to eat sensibly, bathe often, drink plenty of fluids and try to cut down on things that can drive a woman over the edge. An annual visit to the gynecologist for a complete checkup couldn't hurt either, sister.

These are not necessarily the gals you see hanging around the health club doing push-ups. (They may be the ones hanging around the Aries gals doing push-ups . . .) Breaking a sweat in a public place is not her idea of fun, unless of course everyone is buck naked and ready for a rock and roll. Suffice it to say that her idea of regular exercise involves the breast stroke without the swimming pool, and the squat thrust without the exercise mat.

shhh—secrets and fears

Let's open up the astrological closets of a lesbian Scorpio. The areas of her solar chart that contain feelings of guilt, repression, ancestral baggage or family pressure are ruled by shallow air signs. This means that, despite all outward appearances of family ties that bind, she may secretly yearn to travel far, far away from Mom and Dad and forget about any homophobic relatives. But how can she simply forgive and forget like that without ruminating about all the pain and hurt for years to come? Inwardly, she is a carefree soul who allows hurts and slights to roll off her back, but if that secret got out, everyone would want to have a piece of her. (Heck, she should be so lucky!)

Sexually, she would love to flit from clit to clit without so much as a passing glance or another thought, just like a carefree, duplicitous Gemini, but fights with her inner green meanies who tell her not to share even yesterday's meals. Spiritually, she can be more expansive and open-minded than she lets on, but she will go to the racks before admitting it. After all, her power is in her ability to be secretive, mysterious and behind the scenes. Why screw up a perfectly good act?

weaknesses: Are there any?

Old-time astrologers tend to attribute all the worst traits to old Scorpio, and many injured folks say with good reason. Mean, vicious, conniving, selfish and treacherous are just a few traits that come to mind. Of course, for the most part, these negative attributes manifest when she has been absolutely and truly wronged . . . or maybe when she lost out on a job that she wanted but didn't quite deserve . . . or maybe when she woke up on the wrong side of the bed . . . or maybe just for the heck of it.

She can also be too serious and too intense, fixating on things that most normal women would let roll off their backs. So what that the sales clerk didn't say thank you with the proper deference? Forget about the two bucks that the phone company overcharged you. They say that this woman's mind is like a roach motel; thoughts check in but they get stuck inside and rumble around until they die and (hopefully) decompose. Keep waiting, sister.

And in conclusion

For pure intensity and passion, check out the sapphic Scorpio sister. Life with her will never be boring and she will always be in the mood for a little sugar in her cup. Satisfy her sweet tooth and she will stoke your fire. Do I smell something burning?

---

k.d. lang - November 9

Here is a woman with intensity, passion and direction. Born in a small town, she managed through pluck and raw talent to conquer the music world . . . and she conquered it in her way. A serious musician, k.d. is able to bridge country (where she has her roots) with rock and album-oriented rock. Like a true lambda scorpio, she expertly blends in with the musical terrain and changes it subtly yet irrevocably. No compromises, just slow and steady strategic progress. Did I mention that scorpios are sensual, sultry and very sexy? Did I mention that k.d. fits the profile?

Relationships with other signs

While it is better to examine the entire horoscope in any relationship, read ahead to get a general impression of a one-on-one. So you think that Scorpio gals can get along with anyone? Ha!

Scorpio and Aries—For the highly controlled Scorpio dyke, the uncontrollable amazon Aries manner may cause a few tidal waves in the bathtub of business and the sea of love. At work, sapphic Scorpio is not interested in reporting her comings and goings to anyone. Sound familiar, independent Aries? Neither wants to do the drudge work, both want to be the tactical general. In love, there is limited trust but a lotta lust. Okay, okay, you can't have everything, so enjoy what you do have.

Scorpio and Taurus—Happiness reigns for these two sensuous sisters. In business, the sapphic Scorp and gay Bull make a formidable pair: One provides the corporate vision and the other offers stubborn determination and gets things done. In love, both gals have an unquenchable thirst and an overflowing fountainhead. Who gets to sip first, lucky girls?

Scorpio and Gemini—How long can a partnership based only on physical satisfaction and mindplay last? These two sisters may chafe in a business relationship, as secretive and purposeful Scorpio goes her separate way from the frivolous and scattered Twin. In love, a wandering Twin dyke may have her wings clipped by a jealous Scorpio lovergrrl. But there will be plenty to occupy this fly-by-night Twin should she get caught in the Scorpio web.

Scorpio and Cancer—These two highly emotional gals are a tour de force in both business and pleasure. While the queer Scorpion looks for long-term returns on investments, the Crab dyke prepares lunch and hires gal Fridays. Sexually, these two sensuous women not only have similar values but can also rock the walls in their passion. Do I smell bouillabaisse?

Scorpio and Leo—Serious Scorps have a tendency to rain on the optimistic Leo pride parade. In business, many of the proud

Lion's efforts may be denigrated while the lavender Scorp shows her how it's done . . . properly. In love, there may always be something lacking, but it probably won't be sex, thank goodness!

Scorpio and Virgo—The Scorpio-Virgo combination has considerable potential for success. In business, each woman knows her strengths: Strategic sapphic Scorps can plan for a comfortable future while queer Virgins happily take care of the here and now. Same situation in love with the added benefit that sexually, passionate Scorpio mamas can unleash her Virgo's hot pink potential. Lucky girl!

Scorpio and Libra—Sapphic steamroller Scorp will run roughshod over the sensibilities of breezy queer Libra. In business, even Libra's best efforts may be regarded as meager and lightweight by her more serious and intense counterpart. In love, sex manages to register on the Richter scale. It's a shame that the buxom lambda Libra wants to be loved for her mind. Ha, ha, ha. Forgetaboutit!

Scorpio and Scorpio—Any type of one-on-one relationship between two sapphic Scorps will have its elements of deadliness, passion and intrigue. Whew! In business, each one wants the control, and neither quite trusts the other. It's the same thing in love. However, in those rare cases where mutual trust can be developed, there will be enough raging, sizzling lust to set fire to any underbrush.

Scorpio and Sagittarius—There is a greater potential for business success when these two heavenly bodies feel the pull of the other's orbit. Scorpio babes keep their eye on the bottom line while Sag sisters are out forging new opportunities and selling the product. In love, however, these two planets are in entirely different galaxies. One has sex overdrive while the other remains mostly in park. Maybe lesbian Scorp should learn how to play horsie with the gay Centaur.

Scorpio and Capricorn—You can feel the earth move when these two gals connect. In business, they understand each other's needs, motivations, strengths and deficiencies and can achieve unparalleled success. In love, a lesbian Scorp can bring out the best in any repressed Cap gal. If that means dressing her up in nothing but a stick of butter and a bag of sequins, fine.

Scorpio and Aquarius—The intensity of the sweet-and-sour Scorpio mama can become unhinged by the stubborn, yet optimistic Aquarian babe. One is inner directed and the other is outer directed. In business, sapphic Scorps can become compulsively consumed with issues that will simply roll off the backs of Aqueerians. Love is a meeting of water and air. Prepare for a hot thunderstorm and a mildewed aftermath.

Scorpio and Pisces—These two watery women blend well together both in business and in love. Lambda Scorps are concerned with long-term viability and stability of a relationship while the rainbow Fish is eager to please and ready to spoil her partner. In business, one is more strategic and practical while the other is more intuitive and ephemeral. In love, one is passionate while one is romantic. Stand back when these two heavenly bodies collide!

✳

famous scorpios: one a day

Kevin Kline	actor	October 24
Helen Reddy	singer	October 25
Hillary Rodham Clinton	lawyer, politician	October 26
Sylvia Plath	poet	October 27
Elsa Lanchester	actor	October 28
Kate Jackson	actor	October 29
Grace Slick	singer	October 30
Sally Kirkland	actor	October 31
Larry Flynt	publisher	November 1
Marie Antoinette	royal	November 2
Roseanne Barr	actor	November 3
Loretta Swit	actor	November 4
Roy Rogers	actor	November 5
Sally Field	actor	November 6
Leon Trotsky	revolutionary	November 7
Christie Hefner	publisher	November 8
k.d. lang	singer, composer	November 9
Richard Burton	actor	November 10
Demi Moore	actor	November 11
Grace Kelly	actor, princess	November 12
Whoopi Goldberg	actor	November 13
Prince Charles	royal	November 14
Georgia O'Keeffe	artist	November 15
Dwight Gooden	athlete	November 16
Rock Hudson	actor	November 17
Dorothy Dix	suffragist	November 18
Jodie Foster	actor, director	November 19
Bo Derek	actor	November 20
Goldie Hawn	actor	November 21
Billie Jean King	athlete	November 22

women вorn on the cusp

Those born between November 19 and November 25 tend to have a combination of both Scorpio and Sagittarius attributes.

What do you get when you mix the intensity of Scorpio with the expansiveness of Sagittarius? You get a woman who is impatient, involved, determined and has a passion to do good. This gal on a mission is afraid of nothing, so hold on tight when she is charged up or be prepared to be left coughing in the dust.

The sapphic Scorp-Sag possesses a quick mind that can absorb knowledge like a sponge. She is a student of life, able to assemble assorted bits and pieces of information into cogent ideas and theories. With her sharp mind, clearheadedness and ability to argue effectively, she makes a great lawyer, although this is one astrologer who hopes that she would put her tongue to better use than just flapping in the air.

Although feelings of guilt and self-reflection are not high on the list of Scorpio attributes, the little dab of Sag gives this proud mama a conscience and a moral sense of right and wrong. Thems that deserves gets in her book so stay off her list! Conversely, adding a little Scorp to her Sag makes this woman one of the bigger worrywarts of the zodiac.

*freedom is always and exclusively freedom
for the one who thinks differently.*
—ROSA LUXEMBURG

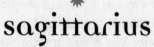

sagittarius

November 23–December 22
The Randy Centaur

Vital Statistics

Element = fire (energetic, action-oriented)
Mode = mutable (goes with the flow, adapts to change)
Ruling planet = Jupiter (the planet of expansiveness and luck)
Ruling house = Ninth (the house of international travel, higher education, the law, philosophy)
Ruling part of the body = hips and thighs
Birthstone = topaz (November) or turquoise (December)
Best day = Thursday
Lucky number = 7, 9
Astral color = purple, gold, red, green
Flower = chrysanthemum
Tarot card = Temperance XIIII (don't rush into anything, get a handle on a situation)

The wise ancient seers dubbed those born between approximately November 23 and December 22 Sagittarius the Archer, the ninth sign of the zodiac.

Sagittarius is the sign of the Centaur, a mythological archer who is half human and half horse. While most mythological monsters were despicable characters, the Centaur is the only one with a few redeeming qualities. Centaurs were the only monsters who were allowed to mix with humans despite the fact that they had a tendency to party too heartily and run amok. (Sound familiar?) Typical scenario: While celebrating the marriage of Pirithous and Hippodamia, one of the centaurs had too much wine and, with jovial orgiastic enthusiasm, attempted to violate the bride. Several others joined in the orgy and a melee ensued resulting in a barbeque au cheval.

General personality and first impressions

What this means is that lesbian Archers have a bit of the feisty animal in them. Many astrology books uncharitably note that Sagittarians physically resemble horses with longish horsey faces and ample thighs. I can personally vouch that Sag gals have the *stamina* of horses and agree with the mainstream that those ample horsey thighs can wrap around just about anyone. But I must draw the line at unflattering horsey facial features. It just ain't true, kids.

This animalistic strain also means that they are not reined in by social convention and are not big on keeping up appearances simply for opinion's sake. These women dress as they please, say what they please and date whom they please when they please. Flannel shirts, loose-fitting jeans and comfortable shoes or hiking boots were made expressly for Sag gals. Dressing up means wearing clean underwear, and a good time can mean anything from a sporting event to a wild international excursion.

Expect your Sagittarian woman to be surrounded by an array of exotic, international galpals collected on their extensive travels. Don't be suspicious if she says that these spicy compadres are really just friends. Trust and believe her; Sagittarians simply cannot lie. It's simply too much trouble to try to remember a cover-up. The truth ultimately comes to light eventually anyway with the disingenuous Sag habit of blurting out the truth accidentally or otherwise.

Sag dykes are not the most graceful of folks and manage to find every darn pothole in town to step into. They set off on adventure, galloping gracefully for a few yards before tripping on their rear hooves. But as silly as they sometimes look, they are the first ones to laugh it off. They are free and comfortable with all their bodily functions. I believe that it was a Sag gal who first coined the phrase "Pull my finger."

career and work

Because Sagittarius is the ruler of the ninth house of travel, higher education, religion, philosophy and the law, sapphic Archers are happiest in careers that give them free range to roam both physically and mentally. They are gregarious souls who need to interact with others and can't be happily confined to a lonely desk job. They are also more egalitarian than most other women and don't rule subordinates by intimidation. In fact, they are more likely than not to be pals with their employees. You will find at least one Sag dyke on every corporate softball team. (See if you can get to home plate with her.)

Don't expect her to play the corporate political game. She cannot lie or suck up to authority. (We leave that to Scorpios.) She will advance based on raw talent, hard work and a gregarious personality. For that reason, she may never make CEO, but she will always be happy with herself and can sleep at night. Thankfully, these gals tend to be rather forward-thinking and a bit prophetic. Her navigation through the corporate maze may have its share of twists, turns and deadends, but she always manages to find the hidden treasure . . . eventually.

A career that involves international travel and/or meeting foreign folks will keep this wandering woman interested and fulfilled. Because she seeks to meet all types of people in all walks of life, she holds no prejudice and can be blunt and outspoken with the truth. This is a woman who can harness any cause close to her heart and take it to the next step. Enlist her help in any of your political and community causes and you will have a maverick.

Other excellent occupations include university professor (or eternal student), lawyer, judge, sales, some type of religious position or anything having to do with animal welfare, especially with their beloved horses. The woman in her late thirties still "working on her dissertation" is probably a Sag. Whatever she decides to do, this sister must be kept busy and, with her flexible and agile mind, she can balance several very different projects at the same time. In fact, she may have two careers going on simultaneously: a corporate gig designed to pay the bills and a sideline for extra pin money, psychological uplift or maybe just for fun.

At the extreme, there are those sapphic Archers who prefer to rely solely on their innate luck (thanks to their ruling planet, lucky Jupiter) and spend their time as professional or not-so-professional gamblers, especially at the horse races. Hopefully they outgrow this phase early in their lives and apply their considerable work skills on more practical enterprises. The rest can be seen begging for quarters on the boardwalk of Atlantic City.

Money

Sag gals don't give a hoot about amassing vast amounts of money to buy and sell souls. We leave that to Capricorns. Archer dykes are far more interested in having loads of fun with their payload. Investments? IRAs? Equity? Where's my dictionary?

Despite this disregard for fiscal prudence, these women manage, through their ruling planet, lucky Jupiter, to be financially successful in spite of themselves. In time they manage to learn a thing or two about saving for a rainy day, but probably not before they've blown a fortune or two.

They are very generous and are considered a soft touch by those in need of a financial infusion. Play her once, play her twice, but this smart girl will catch on soon enough that you are taking advantage of her good nature. The bank will close for all future withdrawals and she will be forced *(ahem)* to take her repayment in kind.

The Sagittarian Home

Their homes have that just-moved-in feel to them because they are never at home long enough to unpack fully and settle in. Don't be surprised if you find her motorcycle parked in the living room surrounded by dirty dishes and old clothes. Charming it's not, but that's probably the worst it could get.

Generally speaking, as she ages and settles down, her home will have a comfortable, lived-in look, chockablock with items and souvenirs from her many travels. The living room will be the center of the house teeming with assorted junk. Despite all appearances, however, she knows where everything is, so don't mess with her messy piles. Don't look at the kitchen; it won't be pleasant. Dishes from prehistoric meals have calcified in the sink and you'll swear that she's cultivating penicillin in the garbage can. I have seen fastidious Virgo faint at the sight of a Sag kitchen. Needless to say, her favorite dinner is reservations . . . or, perhaps an invitation?

These women prefer to live out in the country where they can take advantage of the wide open spaces and lack of prying neighbors. They also have the room to have loads of mixed-breed pets and several bicycles and all-terrain vehicles. Be careful not to step in the unidentifiable brown puddle.

love, sex and relationships

Old-time astrologers call Sagittarius the "bachelor sign" because she has trouble committing to just one woman and may have many brief relationships throughout her life. Whether this is true or not depends upon the placement of other signs and planets in her horoscope. What is absolutely true is that she will have many, many lovers in her lifetime and will enjoy every last one of them.

Because she has a healthy disregard for the opinions of others, she probably came out early in life to her family and friends. Honesty is simply too important to her and keeping up a lie just wouldn't work. Thankfully, most Sags are surrounded by supportive networks whereby they feel little or no negative repercussions.

Once unleashed, lesbian Sags have a lusty, healthy sexual appetite and are very generous in their affections. (Thank goodness for that equestrian streak!) However, they can be emotionally distant, which can be especially upsetting to water sign women (Cancer, Scorpio and Pisces) who live and breathe romance. They are sexual but not passionate, physical but not emotional. Maybe that's why commitment is so difficult for them.

Some friendly advice for keeping your Sagittarian gal from trotting too far afield: Give her room to roam, don't question her about her whereabouts and, by all means, trust her to do the right thing and make the right decisions by herself. There is nothing more frustrating for a sapphic Archer than to have her every move probed. Probe into other things and leave her whereabouts alone. Both of you will be much happier, believe me.

Remember to rub her thighs, especially her inner flanks and tell her how smart she is. Lesbian Archers love to be thought of as brilliant and worldly (maybe even more than being told that they are sexy). However, always remember that action, not talk, will get these girls galloping. Saddle her up and ride your horsie!

friends

Amazon Archers have many unusual and exotic bosom buddies from all over the world. She attracts the most exotic and eclectic crowd because she is so darn interested in everything and everyone beyond her own backyard. Angle for an invitation to any of her parties; it will be an international experience with wonderful and somewhat strange cuisine. (Avoid any hors d'oeuvres with fur.)

Sag gals are the life of any party and enjoy good gay camaraderie. They'll be the ones wearing the lampshades or knocking over the onion dip. They are also the ones with the boisterous but lousy jokes and the loudest, proudest laughs. In a crowded room of quiet Virgos with cocktail napkins and plates carefully balanced on their laps, Sag girlfriends are the ones with cheese sticks up their noses. Ho, ho, ho . . . oops!

A Sag gal will stick by you when all others have given up, not bolstering your ego, mind you, but providing good gay companionship, moral support and a few laughs. Keep her on your A list even though she spilled red wine on your oriental carpet or tracked mud through your house.

family and parents

Archer dykes get along fairly well with family members. This is because they can't abide bigotry and would snarl a few choice words and bolt from the family circle if they were not fully accepted for who they are. They don't tolerate intolerance and are independent enough to cut off any ties that strangle their sense of affirmation and pride. Sapphic Archers usually get along well with siblings as long as they respect one another. In the best circumstances, everybody becomes good, close friends. Ideally, they have happy extended families who enjoy getting together and sharing good times.

As a child and in her formative teen years, she would thrive with a family structure that was less of a dictatorship and more of a democracy. Being allowed to choose her own major in school, for example, would be extremely important to her as would the ability to pick and choose her own friends. Her universal love and friendliness can put her in touch with all sorts of youngsters from all walks of life. Galpals are chosen on the content of their character, not on their glitzy appearance, membership in a particular club or team or bank balance.

Smart parents who understood her feisty nature probably gave her plenty of room to roam as a child and trusted her decisions to build her confidence and independence. Sags are the quintessential "tomboys," climbing trees, scuffing knees and rolling around in the dirt. Petticoats? A clean neck? Forgetaboutit, sister!

communication style

Sag gals are loud, proud and queer when it comes to their communication skills. They love telling jokes (especially ones with grotesque sound effects) and laugh at their own punch lines, painful as they may be.

She treats everyone fairly, is honest and expects the same treatment in return. Woe betide the fool who tries to impose their intolerant attitudes on her! Nuclear fallout is a picnic in the park compared to the venom she can unleash with that divinely sharp tongue. Sagittarian mamas go for the jugular in an argument . . . because they can. Whatever pains you the most becomes fodder for her attack. Amazingly though, once the tirade is over she is back to being her friendly self—no grudges held, at least not by her. Hey, forgive and forget.

Thought your secret was safe with her? Think again! Whether she tries to keep a secret or not, it manages to slip out at the most inappropriate time. Uh, sorry! But before you plan to boil the poor girl in oil, remember that she can't even keep her own secrets secret. So rub warm oil on her instead and be understanding now and more reticent in the future.

Health and Fitness

Sagittarian dykes are very comfortable with their bodies. They are less likely than most other women to have eating disorders and generally eat what they want when they want it. They are big on exercise—hiking, horseback riding, golf and other sports and outdoor activities—and are therefore generally fit and robust. Sagittarius rules the thighs and hips, so most sapphic Archers have well-developed thigh muscles and very huggable hips. Yikes!

Stomach ailments can hit those Sagittarian sisters who do not pack the proper common sense or medication on their life travels. They tend to be experimental gourmands who eat just about anything (bless their hearts) but may have trouble digesting some of the more exotic delicacies that pass through their lips. Meow?

Accidents are big problems for these clumsy gals, so it is advisable for them to take things slowly and carefully. Maybe they should be steered away from more risky sports such as boogie boarding and rock climbing. (Yeah, just try steering them away from anything! They'll probably take it up just to be ornery.) They also have a tendency to scatter their forces by trying to take on too many things at one time. And everything must be completed once it's started! This not only increases stress but can bring on crabbiness, fatigue and, again, accidents.

As they get older, they may bite off more than they can chew, engaging in overly strenuous and risky activities like extreme sports and drag racing, for example. Keep them occupied with less hazardous pastimes. By the time they turn eighty, they should probably pursue more sedate hobbies. . . . Not!

shhh—secrets and fears

Want to help a lesbian Archer throw out the trash in her astrological closets? The areas of her solar chart that contain feelings of guilt, repression, ancestral baggage or family pressure are ruled by sensitive water signs. This means that, despite all outward appearances of a devil-may-care independence, the Sag woman needs a tremendous amount of understanding and tender loving care for her to attain her fully affirmed potential. Sexually, she is an oyster waiting to be devoured. Spiritually, she is apt to be an optimistic dreamer who time and again latches on to hopeless causes. When it comes to her family, she secretly cleaves to her favorite parent who, for good or ill, is a guiding force in her life. But she will pull out her fingernails rather than admit all this. Outwardly, she is a fiercely independent soul who cares little for the restraints of family. Yeah, right.

They are also dreadfully fearful of being thought of as stupid or ill-informed. Quietly, behind the scenes, they are boning up on their vocabulary or reading some old tome that will massage their brain cells and give them an intellectual edge. However, they want to appear naturally brilliant, witty and urbane, especially before they trip on the curb.

weaknesses: Are There Any?

Aside from being more than a little clumsy, sapphic Sags are often the bearers of total, unexpurgated honesty, requested or not. Looking like crap? She'll tell you so, cheerfully and helpfully. Need a confidence-builder because you lost out on that promotion? She'll tell you that you probably didn't deserve the job anyway. And whatever you do, don't entrust her with any important secrets. You'll read about it the next day on the front page of the newspaper. Foot in mouth disease is a Sagittarian hallmark, so learn to live with it if you live with an amazon Archer.

What else? They are lousy housekeepers, preferring to let dust build up to such a degree that it can be lifted off furniture like a sheet of paper. God forbid they should wash a dirty dish . . . or their bra. Once they become comfortable around you they will gleefully fart and belch with abandon. I suppose that it's something to look forward to in your old age and will help save on your gas bill.

And in conclusion

All in all, life with a sapphic Sag is one of adventure, expansiveness and good gay female fun. Enjoy her with all of her peccadilloes. Life would be far too dull without her.

✳

Bette Midler - December 1

The persona of a scrappy, optimistic, loud, honest and friendly Archer is nicely epitomized by the divine sagittarian Bette Midler, who, despite her heterosexuality, has rightfully earned a place as an icon in the gay community. The woman who got her start belting out tunes for patrons of a Manhattan bathhouse has parlayed her Jupiter luck into excellent movie roles and smart career decisions. She's the life of the party who, in her pre-maternal years, happily dressed in outrageous costumes for a laugh. Kind to a fault and comfortable in her body, this gay-friendly Archer sister lives life her way, as all sag gals must. Clumsy? Let's not go there. . . .

Relationships with other signs
Are friendly Sagittarian women compatible with every sign? I advise you to check her entire chart, but until then it is possible to generalize by sun sign. Read ahead, girlfriend, but don't commit yet!

Sagittarius and Aries—The Sagittarius-Aries combination is a meeting of two forthright and independent souls. In both business and love these two rambunctious gals manage to find a happy balance between working as a team and doing their own thing. A sapphic Ram is more forgiving than most of the Archer's undisciplined and informal style while the festive Sag is always available to give her lovergrrl a happy jolt. Watch the voltage, babe!

Sagittarius and Taurus—Sag sisters may be too undisciplined and distracted for patient and directed sapphic Bulls. In both business and love, these two mismatched mamas may be able to find common ground if they are open and flexible. In many ways, these two complement each other, providing zesty oomph where there is placidity and bullish grace where there is Archer clumsiness. But if you are looking for an eternal flame, strike your match elsewhere.

Sagittarius and Gemini—The Sagittarius-Gemini partnership is based on absolute equality and mutual understanding. This works especially well in business, but lacks a certain spark in love. Both of these independent women want to have their choice of lovergrrls and have a problem settling down with just one. Maybe the best we can expect is a quick drop of the anchor before these two steamers pass in the night.

Sagittarius and Cancer—The rollicking lesbian Archer may not be as romantic as the sapphic Crab may like, but in business, these two gals have a good balance of practicality and push. These honest souls can put their best assets to work for the betterment of the team. In love, however, the crude Sag manner may be off-putting to the highly romantic Crab. Just where do you expect to put that finger after it's been in your nose?

Sagittarius and Leo—You can feel the heat when these two fiery gals get together. In business, great ideas abound as each one wants to run out and conquer new territory. (Be sure to hire a capable Virgo to keep the back office running properly.) In love, there is mutual respect and admiration, although it can become more platonic than passionate if both babes fall into a pattern. Be sure to stock up on ticklers to keep things interesting. . . .

Sagittarius and Virgo—These two mamas have a tendency to square off against each other. In business, the lesbian Archer is too scattered and out of control for the conservative and organized sapphic Virgin. In love, one is platonic while the other is clamoring for passion. Sags think Virgos are cheap. Virgos think Sags are wasteful. You tell me.

Sagittarius and Libra—The Sagittarius-Libra combination brings out the best in both gals. In business, reckless, risky Archers can make a better impression when they have their sharp edges smoothed by their lovely Libra partner. In love, the animalistic Centaur can channel her impressive drive into the ever-willing, sweet and sassy sapphic Libra. Practice makes perfect, ladies!

Sagittarius and Scorpio—Independent, honest amazon Archers may feel hog-tied and branded when paired with a lambda Scorp. Their sex drives are not always in sync: Scorps like their lover-grrls anytime, anywhere, anyhow, while Sags have to be "in the mood." Business partnerships have a slightly better chance of success, since Sags enjoy outreach and forging new territories while sister Scorps prefer to tackle sticky issues in the back office.

Sagittarius and Sagittarius—You probably won't find a better pair of bosom buddies than two lavender Sags. The problem here is that neither one is especially disciplined to keep her end of the business from going belly up. Both want the title of Ms. Popularity and don't want to take on the truly unpleasant tasks. In love, sex is about as romantic as a used tampon. How about a warm handshake instead? Wash your hands first, sweetheart.

Sagittarius and Capricorn—A business relationship between the open and hard-working sapphic Sag and her crafty and careful Cap sister has great potential for success. Each one complements the other in terms of strengths and weaknesses, providing excellent one-two-punch effectiveness. In love, lesbian Goats may be too depressing for jolly Archers, and the informality of the Sag manner may be off-putting to conservative Caps. Do beer and caviar mix?

Sagittarius and Aquarius—These two jolly and unorthodox souls have quite a bit in common. In business, they may need to hire a down-to-earth Virgo to keep the books, but these women will be able to grow their business with vision and enthusiasm. In love, there may not be much passion but neither will miss it that much. Pass the popcorn and turn up the TV.

Sagittarius and Pisces—Proud Archers may grow impatient with the idealistic and unrealistic ramblings of a Piscean partner. The sapphic Fish may have her feelings crushed by her Sag sister's brusque and sometimes brutal honesty. In love and in business, these two may run the ship of state aground with conflicting visions and needs. Better to be just galpals.

✳

famous sagittarians: one a day

Erté	artist	November 23
Henri Toulouse-Lautrec	artist	November 24
Tina Turner	singer	November 25
Robert Goulet	actor	November 26
Jimi Hendrix	musician	November 27
Rita Mae Brown	writer	November 28
Busby Berkeley	choreographer	November 29
Shirley Chisholm	politician	November 30
Bette Midler	singer, actor	December 1
Monica Seles	athlete	December 2
Jaye P. Morgan	singer	December 3
Lillian Russell	actor	December 4
Margaret Cho	comedian	December 5
Don King	manager, promoter	December 6
Ellen Burstyn	actor	December 7
Kim Basinger	actor	December 8
Kirk Douglas	actor	December 9
Emily Dickinson	poet	December 10
Rita Moreno	performer	December 11
Frank Sinatra	singer	December 12
Christopher Plummer	actor	December 13
Patty Duke	actor	December 14
Nero	politician, emperor	December 15
Noel Coward	wit, writer	December 16
Tommy Steele	performer	December 17
Brad Pitt	actor	December 18
Edith Piaf	singer	December 19
Kiefer Sutherland	actor	December 20
Jane Fonda	actor	December 21
Lady Bird Johnson	first lady	December 22

women born on the cusp

Those born between December 19 and December 25 tend to have a combination of both Sagittarius and Capricorn attributes.

This sister is a go-getter, blending the best of the Sagittarius oomph and the Capricorn determination. She is more democratic than the garden variety Capricorn and more persevering than the usual Sagittarian. (Think of her as a well-behaved Sag or a relaxed Cap.) The Archer-Goat possesses considerable mental agility and is able to master many diverse subjects spanning many disciplines. Need to know the capital of Mali? Seeking a home remedy for a head cold? Curious about Ken Boswell's batting average in his final year with the Mets? What about Judy Nelson's favorite golf course? I happen to know who to ask.

She is a great worker as well as a great thinker, with an acute eye and a discerning palate—who would have thought? Career options? Try musician or even horse groomer. She is more creative than logical Capricorn and cleaner than sloppy Sag.

It takes a while for these sapphic souls to fall in love and give their heart to another, but once she finds the girl of her wet dreams, it tends to be forever. These proud sisters are considerate travel companions, willing to share a toothbrush—or more—with a warm and fuzzy bunkmate. Consider any type of excursion with them, even if it means booking two singles instead of a double.

A + B + C = success if A = hard work, B = hard play,
and C = keeping your mouth shut.
—Albert Einstein

capricorn
December 23–January 20
The Rugged Mountain Goat

Vital Statistics

element = earth (stability, functionality, process oriented)
mode = cardinal (conceives of and creates change)
ruling planet = saturn (the planet of challenges, difficulties and wisdom)
ruling house = tenth (the house of long-term career, status in the community)
ruling part of the body = teeth, knees, skeleton
birthstone = turquoise (december) or garnet (january)
best day = saturday
lucky number = 6, 10
astral color = garnet, brown, silver-gray, black, sea green
flower = holly
tarot card = the devil xv (learning from life's hurdles, problems that must be faced and can't be ignored)

The wise ancient seers dubbed those born between approximately December 23 and January 20 Capricorn the Goat, the tenth sign of the zodiac.

A Capricorn is not just any type of a goat; it is a mountain goat—the kind with a harder than average life. This sorry old goat spends her life climbing slowly up from the base of the mountain, scavenging for food along the way, eating debris and dried foliage and fighting off enemies. Finally, in a culmination of inner personal strength and exhaustion, she reaches the peak and plants her flag of victory. Capricorns are that rare breed who seem to better with age, hitting their stride and mellowing like fine wine (tart yet sweet, bold yet unassuming). Because she spends most of her life butting her head against obstacles, eventually this smart gal learns from experience. They should think of this when life gives them a zetz.

general personality and first impressions

See that beautiful sad sack over there? The one with the poor posture and the defensive look? She's *got* to be a Capricorn. Depending upon the placement of other planets in her chart, most sapphic Caps come off as serious and conservative. Capricorns also look as if they lack self-confidence. This is quite confusing to other signs who see this particular woman as one with all the looks, abilities and smarts. In truth, she is immensely talented and driven and can achieve anything she sets her mind to. The problem is that along the way, she continually questions herself and her abilities, kicking herself with her mountain goat hind legs all the way up. (But what legs!)

She is deathly afraid of what others think of her and for this reason is probably one of the most closeted signs in the zodiac. Unlike Sagittarians who could give a crap about what anybody else thinks, Capricorn gals measure their success by others' yardsticks. More corporate leaders are Capricorns than any other sign. No wonder.

Although genetics will always play a role in physical appearance, generally speaking Capricorn dykes are short of stature with dark, soulful, expressive eyes that seem to say, "I have seen the troubles of the world. Please be kind to me." The eyes are the windows of the soul; there is nothing else that will give away her complete vulnerability.

I love a woman in a three-piece suit, but on Saturday? This woman chooses her wardrobe from Talbots or Brook Brothers. Cutting edge she's not, but we astrologers prefer to call her look "evergreen." Check out a ten-year-old photograph of her and chances are she's wearing the same sweater. Only now it's tighter, thank goodness.

She is not the most adventurous, outdoor type, preferring to either stay close to home (where it's safer and more comfortable) or traveling to established (i.e., acceptable) resorts or destinations. These ladies are golfers, not necessarily because they enjoy the game but because they can advance their career by playing with the CEO. Just don't ask her to clean the balls!

Many astrology books uncharitably state that Capricorns are tightwads. While they are not lavish Leos, lesbian Caps are more fiscally conservative than downright cheap. They spend all right, but they want to make sure that they're getting their money's worth. Keep that in mind when you ask her for something special and expensive.

career and work
Because Capricorn is the ruler of the tenth house of long-term career and one's status in the community, Capricorn dykes are happiest in careers that afford them status, power and influence. These gals start at the bottom of the corporate ladder in the sub-

basement passing out mail and serving coffee. Through hard work, patience, raw talent, political acumen and a dogged attitude to succeed they eventually manage to rule the roost, tossing out the turkeys and cocks as they amass territory.

When she reaches the corporate starchamber, don't expect her to champion domestic-partner benefits though. She always plays the game according to the established rules and is loath to change the system just when she has succeeded within it. The more enlightened ones, perhaps at the point of retirement, may take a personal stand to change certain things, but don't hold your breath. While she would never vote for Pat Robertson, she may have secretly cast a vote for Ronald Reagan, but let's not discuss that now.

Because they are such sharp observers and quick studies, lesbian Caps are natural "political animals." Thus, they are arguably the most successful women in the zodiac when it comes to winning corporate wars and tussles. They will be incredibly successful in anything they undertake but are best-suited for suit jobs: senior administrator in a major corporation, accountant, banker (especially bank president), financier, *zzzzzzz*. The ultimate job for a sapphic Cap is in politics: She is adept enough to forge alliances with just about anyone no matter how vile and loathsome.

money

This is a woman who knows the value of a dollar, a eurodollar and even a drachma. She is adept at earning and investing her booty and may be one of those few lucky souls who may actually retire comfortably. Splurge is not a word in her vocabulary.

These careful Carols are perpetually worried that the funds will run out and there will be no way to replace them. Oh my gosh, I am unemployable! Undesirable! Without friends for support! Without family for a bailout! Maybe they are without their good common sense. These unrealistic, panic-stricken gremlins can plague them for most of their life. However, this neurotic obsession with cash flow enables her to spend a dollar like it's four and she can stretch the smallest of budgets into a passable safety net. She is a natural planner and will be ready for almost any emergency or setback. Because she is so determined to succeed, the chances that a money drip will eventually turn into a steady flow is almost assured.

The capricorn home

Ethan Allen colonial furniture was made for this gal. An amazon Cap likes the "well-established" look in home furnishings. Look for her in the best neighborhoods, once she can afford it. Until then, she will happily keep a tidy abode in whatever upstanding neighborhood is within her price range. Living beyond one's means is not a workable philosophy for this gal.

Picture a home full of functional furniture, maybe a few antique pieces inherited from an aunt, society and business magazines placed strategically on the coffee table, a large comfy sofa with flowered upholstery and a large dog (probably an Irish setter) sleeping by a roaring fireplace, and I'll show you a home with a sapphic Cap in it.

Check out the state-of-the-art kitchen. One day, she may even hire a cook to break it in. This is the woman who orders out for grilled cheese sandwiches because she works too late to cook for herself. When she does entertain at home, everything is done "right," from the finger sandwiches to the petits fours served on grandma's china. Thank goodness this woman can follow a recipe and never improvises. Unlike a Sag, with this girl culinary practice makes perfect.

Her musical tastes probably tend toward classic oldies rather than Anthrax or Ice T, but of course it depends on what the powerbrokers are listening to. (Let's hope it's not Pat Boone!) Whatever the musical fare, it's probably wafting through the house throughout the day, and it drives quietly contemplative Scorpios crazy.

love, sex and relationships

Mother always says that it's better to fall in love with a rich woman than a poor one. Lesbian Capricorns take this motherly advice to heart and spend a good portion of their youth searching for a well-endowed babe (ah, but don't we all) or one who is well connected and powerful. As ripe old age settles in, your Cap dyke may be tempted by a piece of delicious arm candy, but this is only if her sweet tooth is not fully satisfied at home. Give her plenty of cheesecake and she'll never stray.

Sapphic Caps are not the most sexually experimental folks and may actually come out later than most signs. But don't give this gal short shrift; there is no more considerate lover in the zodiac. She even remembers birthdays and anniversaries with fabulous little goodies. Build her confidence and tell her (truthfully) how wonderful and sexy she is and she will blossom like a rare orchid. Remember, kids, this is a woman who ages beautifully. Treat her well and you'll have some hot stuff to warm you in your old age. Think of Dolly Parton, who happens to be a Capricorn, and dream a dream.

These women are earth signs, which means they have a deep capacity for love, affection and downright dirty sex if they are properly stoked, poked and stroked. Keep this delicious little secret in mind if you set your sights on seducing a Cap gal. Being earth signs, they are also possessive, so if you are one of those flighty undisciplined Geminis or indiscriminate Sagittarians, rein it in or forgetaboutit.

They are not especially demonstrative in public so don't expect a lavish, wet display of emotion and tonguetwisting in front of a gawking crowd. Settle for private pubic affection instead. And for these propitious gals, simply knowing that you care is enough. Let's not get mushy in front of the gang.

friends

Capricorn dykes tend to make friends for life. If her childhood was relatively painless, she'll happily keep in touch with all those boring elementary school friends that most of us eventually outgrow. This is a woman with amazing empathy and patience for bosom buddies who need her advice or a warm, large shoulder to cry on. But, remember, she is not a bank, so refrain from asking for a loan or a few extra bucks to tide you over till your next paycheck. I can already tell you what the answer will be. (Ask a Libra galpal instead; if she has any money, it's yours.)

She is the type of woman who prefers to mingle with "like-minded" (middle of the road) ladies. Don't expect to see her with a raised fist at the next International Dyke March wearing nothing but a tattoo. Instead, she'll be parked at some neighborhood wine bar with a few compadres discussing how a flat income tax makes sense.

At a party, she'll be the one to hang around after everyone has gone to help you with the dishes. Unlike a Sag, she won't break any glasses piling them up in the sink. Hey, you can't help but love her.

family and parents

Generally speaking, sapphic Capricorns tend to have cordial relationships with relatives but may not be especially close to them. Comfort with her sexual orientation may be the deciding factor in whether she will show up at Thanksgiving at all, alone or with her bird. Wise relatives shower her with affirmation and acceptance. Relatives lacking wisdom won't have her to kick around anymore. What a shame. This is the woman who never forgets a birthday or Christmas and who will always remember to call to say hello.

Parental criticism cuts this girl to the quick because Mother and Dad were the first CEOs she had to please. But parental support takes this women to greater heights than anyone ever thought possible. (Paging Dr. Freud!) These are the girls who always brought the teacher an apple and were always chosen to clean the erasers. For these reasons, jealous Leo thugs would get their cronies to beat them up after school and appropriate their gold stars.

These girls are like sponges when it comes to knowledge and habits and they will acquire the behaviors, good or bad, of their surroundings. Maybe it's because they ache to blend in and belong. It is the wise parent who sets boundaries and monitors marketplace trends for her.

communication style

Amazon Caps are careful and politic communicators. They are not gossipers and are generally able to keep secrets, although they have been known to use these tasty morsels to their advantage later on. Her little black book has a list of skeletons in various closets that she wouldn't mind rattling on occasion (all the more reason for folks to empty their damnable closets), so don't stab her in the back. Remember, pal, a doormat, she is not.

These ladies tend to have sharp memories, are fairly perceptive and are thus sought after as professional advisers on everything from career paths to choice of girlfriends. They excel in career advice, but I would stop and think before taking her advice on love. She will always advise choosing the girl in wingtips with a good steady job, which may not be your idea of paradise.

Health and fitness

Lesbian Caps tend to have little nagging aliments throughout most of their lives. They are the ones who get the damn flu every year. This is probably because they have a tendency to run themselves down and work too hard. Rest and relaxation should be mandated on doctors orders for any of these stubborn mountain goats who resist taking weekends off.

Capricorn rules the teeth and skeleton. Smart Cap gals will consult a nutritionist to see if they need calcium supplements and should refrain from eating an excessive amount of sweets— unless they're the human kind. Stress may also cause them to grind their teeth while they sleep. They should retain a good dentist who is always available for emergencies.

These pensive souls can also be prone to depression, melancholia and fatigue due to overwork and general worry. Hey, remember to lighten up, sister, and don't carry the weight of the world on your shoulders.

shhh—secrets and fears

Open up the astrological closets of a lesbian Capricorn and see what you uncover. The areas of her solar chart that contain feelings of guilt, repression, ancestral baggage or family pressure are ruled by feisty, reckless fire signs. There is a part of this woman that aches to break free of convention and moon the establishment but can't because of her fear of failure in other people's eyes. These are also the parts of her life where she feels most vulnerable. Overcompensation can result in impulsive actions that erupt like a blazing fire leaving a trail of charred, ashen remains. Some signs, like Aries, get off on that sort of thing, but Cap dykes would rather eat their young than upset the landscape and cause a scene. Spiritually, she yearns to poke the establishment in the eye and do whatever the heck she darn pleases. (Yeah, I joined a coven. What's it to you, bub?) But somewhere along the way, she loses her nerve and retreats to the tried and truly accepted. Hope, however, springs eternal. . . .

weaknesses: are there any?

Capricorns get a particularly cruel rap in old-fashioned astrology books and we will not shy away from her unpleasant traits in this book either! In addition to bouts of selfishness and self-interest, these women have a tendency to talk too much about their personal troubles and problems. After spilling the beans, they can then become paranoid, suspecting others of using their secrets and weaknesses against them. Ultimately the Cap gal is obsessed in maintaining appearances, her reputation and her possessions, and will go to great lengths to protect herself. Guess Richard Nixon's sign.

Generally speaking, many of them are depressed worrywarts who always manage to find a dark cloud in any silver lining. Particularly mean-spirited types can be induced to perform indiscriminate acts of cruelty, which, if they possess any type of conscience, can eventually lead to pessimism and self-loathing. Truly afflicted types would sell their soul to get ahead and are generally only out for big bucks and the power and prestige money can buy.

One thing is sure, as they get older, they tend to have less to prove and more to move. As kicking kids, they would elbow anyone out of their way. As graying goats, they acquire a sense of propriety.

And in conclusion

Life with a sapphic Capricorn can offer you the best things that life has to offer and a comfortable old age. While she may be serious and uncompromising, it's because she always keeps her eye on the prize. If you want to sip from her cup, be sure to fill it with Dom Perignon.

Dolly Parton - January 19

Like all serious capricorns, Dolly parton came from poor and difficult beginnings and has carefully, tenaciously climbed her way to the top of her profession. she is arguably the queen of country music, and yet, like a careful, pessimistic cap, she dutifully renews her beautician's license every year just in case. Hey, you never know when the fates will cut you down to size. predictably, she's been married to the same man for ages, though this hasn't stopped her from being a favorite figure in the lesbian community.

Relationships with other signs

You don't have to face life alone, sister. While it is necessary to examine the entire horoscope in any relationship, take a look at the following sun sign compatibilities, but proceed with caution.

Capricorn and Aries—Conservative lesbian Caps have a tendency to worry about what capricious Aries dykes are up to. In business arrangements, the proud Ram breaks down barriers while the worrywart Goat sweeps up the shards. In love, the lambda Goat may be too cool for the sapphic Ram's fiery ardor. Neither are great on long-term compromise, so let's agree to disagree.

Capricorn and Taurus—These two earthy mamas are committed to creating and maintaining a profitable and mutually satisfying partnership. In business, they are able to keep their eyes on the prize, combining bullish ongoing effort and perseverance with careful Cap planning. In love, they can build a sturdy foundation for years of happy companionship. So what if their idea of excitement is renting two videos rather than one? There is always enough hot and buttered popcorn to go around.

Capricorn and Gemini—Lesbian Caps have a tendency to rain on the Twin's pride parade. In business, the conservative serious Goat gal can provide the vapid Twin with substance and foundation but may squash her innate enthusiasm and verve. In love, the lesbian Twin's wandering eye may catch a squirt of her lover's tart comments. Caring Caps won't be able to keep this hungry girl nourished on home cooking alone.

Capricorn and Cancer—There is a mutual admiration society created by these two sapphic sisters. In business, both tend to be more conservative and risk averse. It would help to bring on a visionary or risk taker to grow and expand the corporation. In love, however, it is strictly a one-on-one enterprise. Each woman understands her lovergrrl's needs for loyalty and dedication. Sounds like a match made in heaven.

Capricorn and Leo—What does an earthy Cap sister and a fiery proud Lion have in common? If one is impatient and the other selfish, not much. In business, one expects to be complimented on any meager effort while the other is worried that not enough is being done to keep the enterprise afloat. In love, the lambda Cap will not kowtow to the regal missives of her Lion partner but can be plied with a few expensive doodads.

Capricorn and Virgo—The Capricorn-Virgo combination has great potential for success in both business and pleasure. These practical women are both committed to putting their egos aside and giving their best efforts to make any project successful. What they lack in creativity they make up for in perseverance. In love, each one wants to make the other feel like a goddess. Hmmm, what does a goddess feel like?

Capricorn and Libra—Worrywart Capricorn dykes and balanced lesbian Libras are well matched business partners: One overprepares for possible problems while the other offers enthusiasm but little practicality. Together they can tackle just about any obstacle and overcome any problem. In love, however, a jealous Goat can fuel her inferiority complex with a strikingly beautiful Libra lovergrrl. So when will she dump you?

Capricorn and Scorpio—When these two earthy gals meet, there are connections on many levels. In business, they respect each other's opinions and insights and can work as one well-oiled machine to achieve goals. In love, a lesbian Scorp can bring out the best in any repressed Cap gal. She may be the one woman who can get the sapphic Goat to dress in nothing but a Tinky Winky Band-Aid. Pull it off gently . . .

Capricorn and Sagittarius—A business relationship between a practical, conservative Cap gal and a feisty, visionary Archer is bound to be successful. What one can't do, the other can. In love, however, lesbian Goats are very serious about commitment, which can chafe at proud Sag's natural inclination to be unfettered and free. At the same time sloppy Sag may be off-putting to appearance-obsessed Capricorn babes. So if you can't dress her up, keep her naked.

Capricorn and Capricorn—The joining of two Capricorn women is not unlike a merger of two corporations. Prenups and palimony must have been devised by an astute Cap lawyer. In business, each wants to be the primary decision maker and the boss. Each one knows best, each one gets depressed. In love, there is as much fire as a wet match, unless of course one is surrounded by delicious luxuries. Eat, drink, try to be merry.

Capricorn and Aquarius—There is potential for success in a business partnership between a lambda Cap and an Aquarian lass. One can set a firm and secure foundation while the other chases opportunities for global expansion. In love, however, these two heavenly bodies may never collide. Each one needs a jolt to power her source and neither owns a pair of jumper cables.

Capricorn and Pisces—What happens when you pair a serious and practical Capricorn woman with a dreamy gay Pisces? A business partnership would have to be carefully mapped so that detail-obsessed Capricorn will not be driven insane by the meanderings of her lesbian Fish who insists upon rearranging the office in accordance with feng shui. Happily, it is difficult to pry these two apart in love. Spray 'em down every so often so they don't burn to a crisp.

✳

famous capricorns: one a day

Susan Lucci	actor	December 23
Nostradamus	astrologer	December 24
Rod Serling	writer	December 25
Mao Tse-tung	politician	December 26
Marlene Dietrich	actor	December 27
Maggie Smith	actor	December 28
Mary Tyler Moore	actor	December 29
Patti Smith	singer, songwriter	December 30
Donna Summer	singer	December 31
Betsy Ross	patriot	January 1
Barry Goldwater	politician, senator	January 2
Victoria Principal	actor	January 3
Jean Dixon	seer	January 4
Alvin Ailey	choreographer	January 5
Nancy Lopez	athlete	January 6
Bernadette of Lourdes	saint	January 7
Shirley Bassey	singer	January 8
Simone de Beauvoir	feminist, writer	January 9
Sal Mineo	actor	January 10
Naomi Judd	singer	January 11
Howard Stern	radio personality	January 12
Sophie Tucker	singer, red hot mama	January 13
Sydney Biddle Barrows	madam, entrepreneur	January 14
Joan of Arc	saint	January 15
Ethel Merman	singer	January 16
Betty White	actor	January 17
Cary Grant	actor	January 18
Dolly Parton	singer	January 19
Carol Heiss Jenkins	athlete	January 20

women born on the cusp

Those born between January 17 and January 23 tend to have a combination of both Capricorn and Aquarius attributes.

Amazons who possess a blend of Capricorn and Aquarius are perhaps the most evolved ladies of the zodiac. They have a keen business sense and know how to make a dime spend like a dollar and make a dollar last a week. Thrifty isn't the word; let's just say they are not big spenders. Occasionally, though, when the Aquarian energy is particularly strong, they can be persuaded to peel off a bill for an unusual or offbeat cause.

One might think that the unorthodox Aquarian energy does not blend easily with the conforming and fretting Capricorn vibe, but this sister can effect massive global change because she finds the right balance between unstoppable optimism and risk-averse caution. Don't underestimate this feisty woman; you will lose. Think of the Aqueerian Cap as the neutron bomb of the zodiac.

They are the last of the original thinkers, possessing a cool calculating and methodical approach to all sorts of business, and that goes for you too, babe. They are not especially sexual or expressive in love. Check for a pulse the next time she looks like she's sleeping—you never know. They also tend to be difficult partners, obstinate and unbending, ornery and not particularly inclined to share or to kiss and cuddle to make up. Compromise? What planet are you living on?

if I try to be like another, who will be like me?
—yiddish proverb

✳

Aquarius
January 21–February 19
Wet and Wild Women

Vital Statistics

Element = Air (intellectual, conceptually oriented)
Mode = Fixed (fights change, attempts stability)
Ruling planet = Uranus (the planet of surprises and electricity)
Ruling House = Eleventh (the house of friends and large social groups or organizations)
Ruling part of the Body = circulatory system
Birthstone = Garnet (January) or amethyst (February)
Best Day = saturday
Lucky Number = 11
Astral color = Blue, pink, forest green
Flower = carnation
Tarot card = The star XVII (hope, promising outlook)

The wise ancient seers dubbed those born between approximately January 21 and February 19 Aquarius the Water Bearer, the eleventh sign of the zodiac.

Aquarius is the sign of the Water Bearer. Mythology is full of references to the power of water with the Well of Wisdom being the most obvious. Odin, the ruler of Asgard, was apparently a pretty smart guy, but he yearned for more and more knowledge. So much so that he gladly gave up an eye for a sip from the Well of Wisdom. Nowadays it's probably easier just to enroll in a course at City University. Another interesting water reference is Urda's Well, which was so holy that nobody could drink from it, eyeball or no. The three Norns guarded this little drop of paradise: Urda (the Past), Verdandi (the Present) and Skuld (the Future). It is no coincidence that Aquarius is associated with these knowledgeable and wise sources, since she is all knowing (or is it a know-it-all?) and will be the first to tell you so.

general personality and first impressions

Lesbian Aquarians tend to be more passionate about their ideas, personal causes and group goals than about individuals—you included. How many political groups can one woman join? (Don't even try to count.) There she is, defiant fists raised, sweat pouring off her brow and her pounding chest, storming the barricades of homophobic oppression. Take a good look, sister; that's about the most excited you're gonna see this gal get. When the banners are packed away at night, this woman barely musters a heartbeat.

But don't give up hope of gaining the attentions of this spirited babe. There are quite a few ways to get her pulse pulsating. Playing hard to get gets this woman soft and creamy. She loves a challenge, so give her one. Lost causes are her specialty, so pretend that you're one. She is also intrigued by the more off-the-wall characters that most of us cross the street to avoid. Doing something a little unusual now and then may register positively on this babe's wavelength . . . as long as it doesn't involve animal sacrifice.

Expect your Aqueerian woman to be surrounded by unusual and unorthodox girlfriends from all walks of life who she meets through her various groups and causes. She is fairly cutting-edge in appearance herself; blending in is not in her game plan. In fact, she may go out of her way to dress to distress. (Hey, who are you looking at buddy?) Who is that mama with enough body piercings to set off airport security? Chances are she is an Aqueerian.

She is a woman of great possibilities. When she is understood and appreciated, she can reach the highest heights of affirmation, personal strength and impactive usefulness. It should come as no surprise that more U.S. presidents are Aquarians than any other sign. There are major Aquarian thinkers and great inventors as well. Therefore, it is important that she carefully choose the company she keeps and the company she works with to be absolutely sure that her gifts are not squandered or ignored. A steady diet of nay-sayers or homophobes will cause her to question her own judgment, sap her strength and take the spit and fire out of her convictions. If you see her falling into this mental trap, do what you can to rescue her. A genius wasted hurts the entire planet.

career and work

Because Aquarius is the ruler of the eleventh house of friends, large social groups and long-term goals, lesbian Water Bearers are happiest in careers that give them ample opportunity to interact with large groups and great causes. Because she is an air sign, she needs a constant flow of ideas to keep her interested and excited. Clearly a career in politics is possible or teaching, writing, social work or even running a labor union, but don't count out possible career opportunities in the media, the Internet or other new technology; Aquarius is ruled by the planet Uranus, which is the planet of surprises, electricity and new inventions. Needless to say, no matter what profession she chooses, she will be electrifying.

Not-for-profit work gets this woman's blood pumping. What better way to improve the world than by making a small (or not so small) part of it better? There she is handing out foodbank parcels; finding homes for stray cats and dogs; marching for tenants' rights, abortion on demand and free daycare. She is optimism in Doc Martens and a nipple ring.

But a woman can't live on grand utopian plans alone. If she bags the idea of living on the fiscal crumbs of nonprofit work, you may see her in her corporate glory building a state-of-the-art information services department or changing the face of the corporate landscape in personnel. She will be the one to institute partnership benefits and other equal opportunity programs . . . or else! Let's hope that she doesn't hit too many walls along the way. Disaffected Aquarians can be seen rummaging through recycling containers for deposit bottles and mumbling things about international conspiracies and the price of coffee. Rasputin was an Aquarius among other things.

money

Sapphic Aquarians have a very simple and logical attitude toward finances: What is the value of money other than a way to get things done? The revolution, after all, has to be funded. Aqueerian gals don't stock up on dust-collecting tchotchkes or high-priced status items. (We leave that to the Leos.) They also don't perniciously stockpile for the inevitable apocalypse; that's Virgo territory. How can anyone spend good money for a circular vibrating bed when there are people starving in Africa? (After a week of glorious vibratory action, she may say, "Come to think of it, a circular vibrating bed may be a life necessity after all.")

Despite this cavalier attitude toward amassing great fortunes and the guilt associated with lavishly living beyond one's means, there are quite a few wildly successful Aquarians on this planet who seem to manage their money guilt-free. Oftentimes it's because they do remarkable and wonderful things with it that reach and help many distressed, needy people. Oprah Winfrey's success and personal projects come to mind.

The Aquarian Home

The average Aquarian home is wired to the hilt. Their computer and home-entertainment centers enjoy a prominent place throughout this woman's abode. You may even find speakers in the bathroom. This woman of the electronic age even knows how to record one program on television while watching two others. (How else can you watch football when Xena's on the other channel?)

She needs her freedom as much as she needs the air she breathes and for this reason probably owns a selection of all-terrain vehicles for quick escapes. Unlike home-loving Cancer gals, this wild woman may move often and never fully settle down. She may not own a full dining room set for years—snack tables will do just fine. She is also not particularly interested in the fine art of cooking and may happily canoodle on a hot plate and toaster oven before some maternal woman feels the need to come and rescue her from a life of take-out food. In the meantime, however, it's thanks for the TV dinner and please pass the salt *and* ketchup!

Wide open space is not a necessity for her (there would just be more to have to keep clean) and for this reason, she is perfectly content to inhabit the smallest nooks and crannies (yours included) that a real estate agent can locate. However, as much as she will rent a closet, she will never, ever reside in her psychological one, thank goodness. Chances are you will find her in the big city or exurban suburb, close to transportation and wired into the Internet. Ah, home sweet home!

Love, sex and Relationships

"How can I be true to only one woman when there is an entire universe of oppressed women who need my help?" If you buy that line, I have an Aqueerian mama who is looking for you.

These sisters stare soulfully into your eyes and ask you the most personal and impertinent questions about your private desires, dreams and hopes. "How flattering!" you think, as you feel your urges heighten and your body go hot and wet. After a night of unbridled passion (and a few unusual intellectual moves guaranteed to capture your heart), there comes the dawn of clarity. It wasn't you, personally, that she was interested in, it was the concept of you, the thought of you, the philosophy of you, you, you. Now what was your name again? And now it's off to other interesting babes! In this way, she is not that different from the other air signs of Gemini and Libra, but her reasons for behaving in such a way are quite different. She is on a constant quest for the über mama, one who will give her the freedom to pursue her dreams without tying her down or holding her back. Well, maybe you can tie her down occasionally.

This cavalier attitude to commitment and monogamy will drive possessive and jealous water signs (Cancer, Scorpio and Pisces) to the brink of despair. Sometimes she displays a lack of personal empathy in these one-on-one emotional altercations that can make matters worse. She is also not particularly demonstrative or physical, preferring to massage the mind and not the body. Try not to get too touchy-feely with her. She will find it annoying and shrink away like Nosferatu at dawn.

This is not to say that it is utterly impossible to capture the heart of this wild and unflappable woman, but you may want to check your feelings to see why you would even want to. To those intrepid souls, I make the following suggestions: Be independent in your own right and have a few unusual thoughts on hand for a rousing discussion. Secretly e-mail her a mysterious scavenger hunt and make sure that you are the final delicious prize. Join her in her causes and, finally, grow a very thick skin. Sister, you'll need it.

Friends

Aquarian gals tend to gravitate to unusual types, the more unusual the better, and may become bored with your average, blend-in-with-the crowd sweet Sues. That is not to say that this sister travels with a menagerie, but, generally speaking, her gal-pals are a motley crew of freethinkers and great minds that come in assorted packages.

Aquarian lesbians tend to be loners at the end of the day, preferring to go home alone with their thoughts rather than engage in shallow dialogue and a blow-by-blow recap of the evening with a roommate or partner. But don't think of her as a fair-weather friend. She is, in fact, one of the most loyal women around—once you've earned her friendship. She will always make herself available to a friend in need, especially if that compadre is seeking advice or direction. And it is very well-thought-out advice too.

family and parents

In the best of circumstances, Aquarian dykes are great pals with her parents and siblings. This is when they give her freedom and respect her opinions, no matter how inane. The wise parent will set up careful but not altogether restrictive boundaries for this little lass, giving her the impression that she has more control over her environment than she may actually have. Toys that spark her curiosity and pique her active mind are mandatory to keep her occupied and out of trouble.

Even as young things, these girls were challenging school authority and instigating lunchroom revolutions. Storm the cafeteria kitchen; I hate liverwurst! However, she may become easily bored with classroom mediocrity, unchallenging schoolwork and the idiots who are teaching her. It is then possible that she may opt out of the formal educational system entirely, deciding instead to seek her knowledge from firsthand life experience. Unless she has some fixed or earth signs somewhere in her horoscope, this dramatic move would be a mistake since it prepares her for nothing more than dilettantish chitchat at dinner parties and a life of low-level, deadend jobs.

My advice to a parent of a proud Aquarian girl: Encourage her to be herself and explore her feelings, and by all means accept her many friends. If you can't say something nice about her half shaved head, try complimenting her on her initiative and trendy creativity.

communication style

Think of her as Clark Kent with X-ray eyes and a streak of superhuman strength when she gets going. Aqueerian women speak with passion, especially when they embrace a cause. They are the ones hoisting the rainbow banner high at every pride march. She is logical and can present a cogent, well-thought-out argument designed to sway the masses. This woman is a creative thinker, able to view a situation with unique perspective and put her own unorthodox spin on it.

These proud gals have an almost obsessive desire to search for and seek the truth, no matter how buried or how painful to excavate. And she will stubbornly take a pickax to it until it's unearthed, examined and catalogued. Secretive sisters such as Scorpios bleed under this type of scrutiny but other, more open babes such as the fire signs (Sagittarius, Aries and Leo) flock to her and demand inspection. It should be mentioned that, while she is greatly interested in exposing your particular secrets to the immediate world, she is not quite as motivated to expose her own. Ask her a direct question and you may get a worldly platitude as the evasive answer. Some call this obvious ploy a mind game, others call it self-protection with a little bit of hypocrisy sprinkled in for good measure. Who am I to judge?

Her sharp and expansive mind needs to be harnessed and focused. Otherwise, she can obsess on the big picture and stumble on the details. For this reason she can be deemed inefficient and flaky, running off to do battle without the proper armament and protection or unable to react quickly to setbacks. For obvious reasons, these gals make better politicians than generals. It is interesting to note the many Aquarian U.S. presidents and how two in particular seemingly naively took on altruistic causes and succeeded admirably, despite the risks of forging a country, winning a civil war and emancipating slaves.

Aqueerians tend to be more liberal in their outlook and can't abide cleaving to outdated dogma or following repressive traditions under the guise of "blind faith." For this reason, they tend to be among the most unreligious women you'll ever meet, replacing what they will refer to as illogical superstition with clear practical scientific thinking. However, throughout all these heavy issues, this gal possesses a remarkably robust and healthy sense of humor that can range from the subtly intellectual to the hopelessly raucous.

Health and Fitness

Aquarius rules the circulatory system and Aquarian dykes should be careful of any systemic infection caused by stress, general neglect or careless habit. Under adverse circumstances, she may catch a cold or flu once a year or may acquire a nagging virus that simply has to work its way through and eventually out of her system. Slow down, girlfriend, and learn to care for yourself as much as you care for the great unwashed. Moderation in food, drink, exercise and general exertion is greatly advised, as well as a daily bath or shower . . . *ahem.*

Despite this possibility, and unless her chart is adversely afflicted, an Aquarian dyke seems to be blessed with a healthy constitution that can withstand hours of grueling picketing in the rain, meals on the hoof and screaming matches with fascist demonstrators. A good rubdown now and then will ease her aching muscles, get the blood flowing, build up her constitution and make both of you feel pretty darn good.

shhh—secrets and fears

What lurks in the astrological closets of many Aqueerians? The areas of her solar chart that contain feelings of guilt, repression, ancestral baggage or family pressure are ruled by solid earth signs. Outwardly, she is a sexual bon vivant who upends the basic trust and connection between lovergrrls. But in those secret places of her psyche, she craves connection and one-on-one satisfaction and physical refreshment. Somewhere in her inner core, she desires stability, loyalty and monogamy, but sometimes it gets lost in all the static. Spiritually, she is not as iconoclastic as one would think. In fact, under those layers of suppression, she realizes that logic alone cannot account for the miraculous and spiritual wonders of the world. When it comes to her family, she will always be there for Mom and Dad, even if it pulls her across continents to help them out. And somewhere in the recesses of her mind, she craves a stable home life. Go figure.

"But let's avoid these sensitive, highly irrelevant subjects, shall we? They distract from far more important and universal needs and injustices." Yeah, sure.

weaknesses: are there any?

Beside being a cold fish in bed, these Aquarian mamas may become self-serving, self-aggrandizing iconoclasts who don't care a whit about the oppressed but use their injustices to build a career and reputation for themselves. The libertarian philosophy of Aquarian Ayn Rand seems to fall into this category.

Aquarian mamas are also not particularly sentimental or good at remembering dates, your birthday or any special occasion included. Sensitive water signs (Pisces, Cancer and Scorpio) are devastated by this inconsideration but, believe me, it is done without malice. It is also done without thought. So, as you sit there in your party best, waiting for your guerrilla grrl to come home and celebrate your anniversary, remember that she may be caught up in the fever of the moment trying to change the world or upend the current system of oppression. Your private little bash will have to wait . . . and wait . . . and wait.

All of the above, of course, is the extreme, and one would have to look at the entire horoscope before you send this girl to the far reaches of your social calendar or back to her hovel for penitence. Hey, I thought patience was a virtue.

And in conclusion

Life with an Aqueerian will take you to the highest heights of self-affirmation and glory, if you are able to grab on to her wings and hold on tight. This independent, opinionated sister can provide you with hours of stimulating conversation, dry wit and a night of wonder to reminisce about for years to come.

Ellen DeGeneres - January 26

How do you reach multitudes to change people's perceptions and bring people to a new level of acceptance and understanding? A highly wired Aqueerian knows that television is one great, global way to go. Ellen DeGeneres is a remarkable woman who fulfilled her sapphic Aquarian urges to reach out and change the world for the better as best as she could and on her own terms. But, like a fixed lambda water bearer, she is not especially forthcoming with her own deeply personal feelings. Rather, she proudly hoists the rainbow banner, gets the crowds going and then disappears into the background seeking privacy. Typical Aqueerian . . .

Relationships with other signs

Aqueerians seem to get along with everyone. Or so they think. It is advisable to check out her entire horoscope, but take a short-cut for now and check out these general sun sign compatibilities. Proceed with caution, girlfriend.

Aquarius and Aries—Aqueerians and sapphic Aries can form very stable and successful partnerships in business and in love. The Aquarian sister infuses her Ram with vision to take any project to the next important step while the Aries woman infuses her partner with confidence and gumption. In love, the energy and stamina of both women keep them interested and . . . amply fulfilled.

Aquarius and Taurus—Aqueerians are on the move while Bull babes are more placid. In business, the stubborn determination of both women may create conflict. Lesbian Aquarians are committed to the common good while sapphic Taureans want what they want when they want it. In love, one may seek excitement across the world while the other waits at home, watching TV and eating twice her weight. Guess who is who.

Aquarius and Gemini—The Aquarius-Gemini combination works well in business and in love. In business, both gals are visionary and expressive (be sure to hire a capable Cancer to keep the back office running smoothly and efficiently). In love, these women are agile gymnasts. There is no telling what creative positions they can assume.

Aquarius and Cancer—Close-working partnerships between these two divergent women will have its ups and downs. Lambda Aquarians are simply too independent to have to account for their every move, and sapphic Crabs simply need to know every little detail. In love, one's exclusive passion is another one's cloying nuisance. Oh well, there's always canasta.

Aquarius and Leo—The Aquarius-Leo combination will have its points of contact and moments of drift. On the one hand, both sisters may be so independent that they may operate beyond each other's spheres of influence like great ships passing in the night. On the other hand, there may be a wonderful meeting of the minds and a powerful, positive connection. I've rarely seen it, however.

Aquarius and Virgo—In business, the optimistic and expansive Aquarian dyke adds power and passion to the quiet application of lambda Virgo. In love, however, the Water Bearer is too independent for the home-loving sapphic Virgin. There could be a lot of lonely nights when one is out ranting and raving while the other fretfully keeps the home fires burning to ash.

Aquarius and Libra—There is a wonderful meeting of the minds when these two airy gals get together. In a business relationship, both are happy to socialize and strategize, but neither is particularly interested in filing or tending to the nitty gritty day to day. In love, they court each other with their suggestive banter and sweet and sassy repartee and they sometimes put their tongues to even better use.

Aquarius and Scorpio—These two gals operate in separate galaxies and it is doubtful that their exploratory missions will record any evidence of life. In business, Aquarian dykes don't sweat even the big stuff while sapphic Scorps can become consumed with every little issue. Love is like a bucket of ice water: a refreshing drink if you're that thirsty but unpleasant to bathe in.

Aquarius and Sagittarius—A certain magic is in the air when these two unorthodox sisters hook up. In business, each one offers new solutions to old, intractable problems. Neither one is a prima donna and is ready to pitch in and help out wherever necessary. In love, each one demands their freedom to choose. Let's hope that they choose each other.

Aquarius and Capricorn—There is potential for success in a business partnership between an Aqueerian gal and a sapphic Cap. One plans for expansion and global strength while the other is content to slowly build the business brick by brick. In love, however, it may not be a slice of paradise. Both need an energizer for their engines and neither has the wherewithal to oil the motor.

Aquarius and Aquarius—When two Aqueerian sisters get together you either have a trade union or an insurgency or both. It is unlikely that these two girlfriends will ever see eye to eye in business. Both are right, both are ready to fight. No one wants to do the books or the filing. In their book of love, it is hard to find a chapter on lust. Read the chapter on cold companionship instead.

Aquarius and Pisces—A lambda Aquarian may upset her Piscean woman's applecart of happiness with her reckless disregard for the feelings of others. In business, both tend to be optimists, which means no one really wants to deal with the ugly and boring day to day. In love, great care must be exercised so that the romantic fire set by Pisces gets stoked every so often by the more down-to-earth Aqueerian.

famous aquarians: one a day

Geena Davis	actor	January 21
Linda Blair	actor	January 22
Chita Rivera	performer	January 23
John Belushi	comedian	January 24
Virginia Woolf	writer	January 25
Ellen DeGeneres	actor	January 26
Mozart	composer	January 27
Colette	writer	January 28
Oprah Winfrey	talk-show host, producer	January 29
Vanessa Redgrave	actor	January 30
Tallulah Bankhead	actor, columnist	January 31
Princess Stephanie of Monaco	royal	February 1
Ayn Rand	writer, philosopher	February 2
Gertrude Stein	writer, philosopher	February 3
Betty Friedan	feminist	February 4
Jennifer Jason Leigh	actor	February 5
Zsa Zsa Gabor	celebrity	February 6
Gay Talese	writer	February 7
James Dean	actor	February 8
Mia Farrow	actor	February 9
Laura Dern	actor	February 10
Tina Louise	actor	February 11
Abraham Lincoln	president, lawyer	February 12
Kim Novak	actor	February 13
Molly Ringwald	actor	February 14
Susan B. Anthony	feminist	February 15
Sonny Bono	singer, politician	February 16
Michael Jordan	athlete	February 17
Helen Gurley Brown	writer, publisher	February 18
Prince Andrew	royal	February 19

women born on the cusp

Those born between February 16 and February 22 tend to have a combination of both Aquarius and Pisces attributes.

With the combination of Aquarian aloofness and Piscean dreamy romanticism, the Aqueerian Fish can be difficult to pin down emotionally. They can be rather cavalier in friendships, promising gal pals the world while delivering a can of rotting compost. Just because they are occupying the space next to you doesn't mean that they are there with you. They have active minds that always seem to be focused on the next project or unattainable goal. Lovergrrls are advised to maintain a very independent and self-confident outlook to maintain their sanity and self-respect. Interestingly, while it is difficult for these gals to find the right woman, once they do they are very contented kittens and will go to great lengths to keep the relationship hot and buttered.

These sisters are very honorable and forthright in business and tend to be very successful in any undertaking, which they are happy to tell you about ad nauseum. This drive for power and money is probably because they love luxury, and luxury doesn't come cheap! At the same time they can be incredibly impractical (Pisces) and a bit peculiar in their tastes (Aquarius). I knew there had to be someone who would buy that secondhand nuclear waste bin plant holder and cup warmer. . . .

when life does not find a singer to sing her heart,
she produces a philosopher to speak her mind.
—Kahlil Gibran

pisces
February 20–March 20
Rainbow Fish

Vital Statistics

element = water (fluidity, emotionally oriented)
mode = mutable (goes with the flow, adapts to change)
Ruling planet = Neptune (the planet of mysticism, illusion,
delusion, creative and foggy thinking)
Ruling house = twelfth (the house of secrets, spirituality and
personal prisons)
Ruling part of the body = lymphatic system, feet
Birthstone = Amethyst (February) or aquamarine (March)
Best Day = Thursday
Lucky Number = 12
Astral color = white, pink, emerald green, black
flower = violet
Tarot card = The Moon XVIII (subconscious, fantasy, deception)

The wise ancient seers dubbed those born between approximately February 20 and March 20 Pisces the Fish, the twelfth sign of the zodiac.

There is a lot of cheap talk around town about the arrival of the Age of Aquarius. The fact is, sisters, that we are still traveling through the Piscean Age and will be until around the middle of the twenty-first century. The Piscean Age began around the time of the birth of Jesus Christ whose birthday was actually reputed to be in March and not in December. (Certain religious experts contend that early Christians moved Christ's birth to December to compete with Apollo's birthday celebration, but that's another story.) Pisces is the sign of the fish and Christ is symbolized by a fish (and a lamb—the sign of Aries that also falls in March). It's not a coincidence, kids. And by the way, the magi were astrologers who consulted the stars and realized that a unique celestial event was happening. That's why they set out to find this new king of the Jews. Ah, the power of astrology!

general personality and first impressions

What this means is that Pisces enjoys a special place in the zodiac and the sapphic women born under this sign hold a special place in our hearts. She is a mystical delight, romantic, spiritual and ephemeral. Some might even say crazy, false, shallow and delusional, but that's usually when her chart is adversely afflicted. You'll recognize her by her soft flowing garments, scarves and loopy, excessive jewelry and can find her haunting tea salons, new-age bookstores and little knickknack shops. This is a woman who believes in ghosts, karmic fate, things that go bump in the night and the power of the occult, tarot and astrology. Obviously, a woman after my own heart.

Pisces rules the twelfth and final (highest) house of the zodiac. This house system goes from the very basic first house—beginnings, physical appearance—and works up the ladder of personal needs to the spiritual twelfth house of religion, the soul and outreach. It houses our psychological closet—the last bastion of homophobia and personal prisons—as well as our hidden enemies. At her best, the twelfth house native is a gloriously affirmed soul. At her worst, she is a prisoner of her own fears, neuroses and prejudices.

This is a woman who generally gives more than she expects to receive. She lives and breathes romance and will look for a silver lining in every cloud of despair. Some, more practical gals (like sister sign Scorpio) chalk this up to hopeless naïveté or, perhaps even worse, lunacy, but don't sell this proud lass short. Is she crazy? Ha! Crazy like a fox! And such a fox! While most of us manage to step in every pothole of life (well, most Sagittarians at least . . .) the lesbian Fish views the world through rose-colored glasses and always manages to survive unscathed the hottest fires of hell. Even if you have trouble believing in guardian angels, you can't help but be impressed by this sapphic gal's protective armor.

You can recognize a Piscean dyke by her placid, bedroom eyes and full face with luscious lips that ache to be caressed and kissed. She is, without a doubt, one of the sexiest babes in the zodiac, but like her mutable sister sign Gemini, overdelivers in allure what she underdelivers in fidelity. But we'll get to that later. . . .

career and work

Pisces is a water sign and is ruled by Neptune, the god of the seas. This means that she can achieve great success in any "liquid" profession: lifeguard, oil worker, sailor or fisherwoman. She is not a corporate animal; we leave the political machinations to the strategic Scorpios and calculating Capricorns. If the fates are kind (and who wouldn't be kind to this believer in fate?), she will wind up on a career path that enriches her psyche, expands her dreams and beautifies the world all at the same time. Expect to see her involved in some creative profession such as fine art, photography, writing, choreography or dance (Pisces does rule the feet) or as someone on the spiritual plane such as a seer, faith healer or member of the clergy. Sort of like a fisher of souls.

Other, more down-to-earth types, will venture into the healing professions as a nurse or physical therapist. Some may gravitate to work in prisons or with shut-ins or for myriad community causes. The Piscean twelfth house is a hotbed for confined places and hidden nasties but it is also a place of self-actualization and personal renewal. It is through this difficult and sometimes thankless work that she achieves her place in heaven. No matter where she winds up in her profession, there will always be a little bit of the do-gooder in her. How about doing a little good in her?

money

Lambda Fish are not in their professions for the ego or the power. And I suppose it goes without saying that they are not in it for the money. For this reason, they always seem on the edge of financial disaster, scraping their dusty pennies together at the end of the month to pay the rent or trying to sponge a meal off a more well-heeled gal pal whenever they can. Unless there are enough practical elements in her birth chart, these mighty aphrodites will have to marry the right (read: loaded) woman in order to gain fiscal solvency. My advice to these financially capricious souls: Always, always, always cleave to a well-endowed benefactress. Lord knows, we all try!

Piscean women always want to live beyond their means and

generally have no concept of money and financial prudence. This behavior would normally drive fiscally responsible women, such as Capricorn, to drink and drugs. Of course, such excesses would be an added bonus for sapphic Fish who, *ahem*, have been known to overindulge in escapist recreational pastimes.

This gal goes on spending binges, especially when she is blue. She is the type to splurge on luxuries and scrimp on necessities. Spending money in a grand manner gives her a sense of control and power over her surroundings. Of course, as with many things in this mama's life, it is an illusion and can get her into even deeper water in the financial ocean she may drown in. But, remember, this lady is harbored under the sign of the Fish and, eventually with a bit of luck and some calm seas, she will swim to safety.

The piscean Home

You'll recognize a sapphic Pisces home by its quiet good taste. She abhors the coarse and the common so forget about early bordello, crushed red velvet accoutrements or high-tech metal pipe couches or lamps in the shape of Elvis. Everything is *so* comfortable and lovely, down to the fresh flowers, well-styled wooden furniture and comfy pillows that it's almost a throwback to a simpler time. Chances are she'll have a garden or, for those city gals, windowboxes full of flowers and herbs. Her decorating style can also be described as "imaginative" with little inspired touches that can make old fabric or a worn piece of furniture an *Architectural Digest* standout.

Her home is her refuge and any area of water (hint: bathtub) an especially prized retreat. It is her place to unwind, contemplate and rejuvenate. Her bathroom is more than likely the loveliest part of the house with scented soaps, candles galore and maybe a little inflatable waterproof pillow to rest her head (or yours) during bathtime. Wise lovergrrls will remember to pack the rubber duckie for long weekends and intimate nights.

Love, sex and Relationships

Sugar and spice and everything nice, that's what Piscean babes are made of. They exude sexuality and can use it to their advantage with hapless and naively unprepared lovergrrls. These gals are natural and graceful and make it a point to master the art of lesbian sex. I think of them as black widows ready to snare unsuspecting little flygirls into their alluring webs, but this may be too harsh a comparison. They are not evil ladykillers. They are just naturally sugary and juicy and ready to share their sticky sweets with almost anyone. But they expect romantic reciprocation for their efforts. Pillow queens need not apply, unless of course they're paying for the flavored oil, the champagne and the first-class air tickets to the islands . . .

The fact is that this woman aches for a faithful relationship. She is in love with love and can't wait to find a lovergrrl with whom to share her dreams of blissful happiness. She loves children and avidly seeks a partnership with a like-minded woman. If you settle in with a sapphic Pisces, expect the pitter-patter of little feet within the first two years, and I don't mean cats! Her naive optimism is often put to the test in relationships and, as much as she desires a forever, she is a mutable sign who knows when forever simply means for the time being.

Lesbian Fish have a tendency to believe everything that you tell them, especially when they are in the throes of ecstacy. Little sweet nothings become golden nuggets, so be careful of promising her the world; she'll expect it the next day by special delivery. In return, she will love you, warts and all, providing you with devotion and sweetness.

However, with her overactive imagination, any curl of your lip or wayward glance can be blown way out of proportion. She imagines all sorts of infidelities, even when none exist, which can drive a wedge between even the most committed partners. In her quest for perfection, she tends to sip from several cups at one meal. Whether this means that she happily joins in a three-some, foursome or twelvesome, or is content to graze quietly from bush to bush, depends on other planetary placements in her chart. Suffice it to say that she is searching for the perfect grape to peel and suck and must continue to taste from every vine to maintain her highly educated and discerning palate.

friends

This is a woman who needs other women around her most all the time. She will do anything that is within her power to help a friend in need. But don't count on her to join you in battle. This is a gal who would rather make love than war. Unlike headstrong Aries, she will strive for compromise or acquiese when an opponent looms too large. Don't call her afraid, call her an eminently wise survivor.

She wants desperately to be liked and will go out of her way to please. The loyalty that she seems to lack in love relationships she amply compensates for in friendships. The lambda Fish is probably one of the most endearing friends one could ever have, defending and befriending even the most dislikable cur. ("Hey, maybe she's just having a bad year?") It does sometimes seem that she likes just about everybody no matter what their politics or personal habits are. This especially annoys more particular signs, like Capricorn.

family and parents

Like other water signs, Piscean babes seem to be especially close to their family, particularly their dominant parent. The risk here is that if this parent is selfish or manipulative, she will be a marionette to Mom's or Dad's puppeteer. Hopefully there comes a time when she wakes from her stupor and realizes that life and affirmation are passing her by. There has to be some point where she breaks free from family restrictions and sets her own course to seek her own happiness and personal fulfillment. Heck, that doesn't mean that she should break off all ties; she can still show up for holiday dinners and festive family occasions. Hey, don't forget to bring your girlfriend!

These charming lasses were very extremely popular as youngsters. Affable, kindhearted and helpful, they aroused the protectiveness of otherwise combative girls such as Aries and were invited into even the most exclusive cliques courtesy of selective Scorpio. However, Pisces dykes were (and are) extremely sensitive souls and any rejection from a desired group was (and is) treated like a sharp sword piercing her heart. For this reason, she tended to swim from group to group and, as such, had (and still has) a collection of galpals that defies definition and category.

She herself was hard to categorize as a young guppie, either roughhousing with the tomboys, acquiring ripped shorts and bruised knees, or hanging around the sidelines with the girlie girls in their white lacy anklettes and moist undies. Hey, what day of the week is it?

My advice to a parent of a proud Piscean girl is to allow her to find her own voice but be prepared to give her a guiding hand and steer her away from those who would lead her into dissipation or destructive distraction. Buy her a deck of tarot cards to help her channel her intuitive gifts.

communication style

Lesbian Pisces are among the most chitchatty gals of the zodiac. It is said that they talk too much, going on and on about nothing, asking far too many questions and giving far too many answers. It is said that in lieu of talking to anyone in particular, she will happily talk to herself, being inattentive and insensitive to the general flow of conversation. (When she starts to answer her own questions, I would excuse myself from the room.) Some, more proprietary women would consider this behavior impolite or simply odd, but Pisces means no harm. She is just a naturally bubbly babe and sometimes the bubbles go to her head. Please be kind and understanding of this foggy soul.

She tends to talk to the general, spiritual and otherworldly, not to the nuts and bolts. Her nebulous ruling planet, Neptune, has trouble focusing on the details and the clever strategies. For this reason, she seems to waver and waft. It may be hard to pin her down in an argument. Try just pinning her down instead and forget about who said what.

Health and fitness

Sapphic Pisces are more emotional than physical and tend to internalize worry and anxiety until they manifest in physical ailments. For the most part, Pisces can lead healthy lives but must take care not to let their emotional baggage pile up and box them in. At the extreme, they can be plagued by melancholy thoughts that lead to addictive, unhealthy outlets for relief. Addictions run the gamut, from nymphomania (my personal favorite) to chocoholism to alcoholism to drug addiction. (Because Pisces rules the feet, I can also picture them with a foot or shoe fetish, but that's another story . . .) In the throes of depression, when those little voices of doom turn up the volume, it is best to seek a bosom buddy rather than a bottle to pull one through the morass.

These gals are restless and on the go, burning up excess calories as nervous energy. You probably won't see them puffing, pulling and pushing to the barks of a personal trainer, but you might see them nervously pacing around the gym looking for someone—anyone—to talk to.

With all their nervousness and internalizing, they can become prematurely gray. Physical afflictions can also include anything having to do with the feet: bunions, toejams, athlete's foot and corns. Remember this groaner: A healthy foot makes a happy ruler.

shhh—secrets and fears

Are there tales to tell about the contents of the astrological closet of a sapphic Pisces? The areas of her solar chart that contain feelings of guilt, repression, ancestral baggage or family pressure are ruled by unemotional air signs. This means that, despite all outward appearances of deep caring and concern, this lady of the lake unfathomably and secretly yearns to fly away from tight engagements and live her own vagabond life. But this dredges up feelings of guilt, recriminations and extreme loneliness. Inwardly, she yearns to hit the highway in a surge of unfettered freedom and liberation. Maybe that's why some of these gals travel so much and live in so many different places.

Sexually, this mama may be less emotionally inflamed than she lets on and is more concerned with a physically beautiful piece of arm candy rather than a substantial, fully developed woman with exciting ideas and ill-fitting dirty overalls. Spiritually she is more rebellious than one would think but would rather walk on hot coals than publicly question long-held, generally accepted religious beliefs. However, somewhere along the line, she would consider selling her soul to the devil just to get a true taste of fire and brimstone. Talk about a hot babe!

weaknesses: are there any?

While not all Pisces are paranoid, neurotic, careless, illogical or users, many old-time astrology books list these traits as a given. Truthfully, it depends on the other positions of the planets in the chart. But as long as we are reviewing weaknesses, let's add infidelity, inconstancy and using sex as leverage to the list. Lambda Fish are not especially careful with their own or other people's belongings and can borrow and lose things with abandon. They may also just "borrow" things without asking because they simply *need* them!

They are not malicious souls and do not mean to hurt others. It is probably because they are prisoners of their own personal demons that sometimes their behavior is self-destructive, uncontrollable and hurtful. Be forgiving of her peccadilloes and concentrate instead on her liberating imagination, sense of fun and romance and her lofty spirits. Take her to the highest heights but don't forget to plumb her depths along the way.

and in conclusion

All in all, life with a sapphic Fish is one of romance, fun and frolic. If you build her confidence and don't give her reason to worry, she will provide you with a life of love and mystery!

Relationships with other signs

Before you give your heart and soul to just any woman, please check her complete horoscope. In the meantime, read the following sun sign comparisons to pique your curiosity.

Pisces and Aries—There will have to be considerable compromise in any Pisces-Aries partnership. First, Aries dykes have to promise not to denigrate their Piscean partners' hopes and

---

Chastity Bono - March 4

Lambda fish tend to come off as vulnerable, sensitive and romantic. sounds like sapphic chastity Bono fits the profile. chastity knew her sexual orientation at an early age, but, wedged between the two large personas of her famous parents, she took many years to come out to mother, cher, and father, sonny. Thankfully she did so and maintains a close relationship with her family—very important for piscean sisters. pisces have an urge to serve and so does chastity. As spokesperson for GLADD (the Gay and Lesbian Alliance Against Defamation), she can fulfill her piscean karmic destiny to do good for our community. Thank goodness!

---

dreams, no matter how foolish, impractical and naive they may sound. Second, rainbow Fish must not make their sapphic Rams feel guilty because they want to spend the entire weekend watching sports. They say love conquers all. Yeah, right.

Pisces and Taurus—While Pisceans are not the most practical gals, they have a certain innate appeal to down-to-earth Bulls. In business, one dreams up all sorts of new and wonderful goals while the other provides all the practical application needed to get the job done. Romance is high on the list in love. How often can a couple couple? You'll lose count in this partnership.

Pisces and Gemini—Intuitive, proud Pisces may be too cloying for the flirtatious and independent sapphic Twin. In business, neither one seems to be able to get a project off the ground or on a direct course. Both are content to do lunch and plan receptions. In love, one is seeking a soulmate while the other prefers to sample from a field of lovely choices. Let's guess who is who.

Pisces and Cancer—These two watery girlfriends make for a wonderfully warm and wet tag team. In business, they seem to work in sync with one compensating for the other's shortcomings. Sometimes their intuition alone can lead them to success. In love, they are perhaps the dreamiest couple in the entire zodiac. Some women have all the luck!

Pisces and Leo—Rainbow Fish will have to exert considerable patience and attention on the glory-grabbing lambda Lion. In business, Pisces babes want to decorate the office and spend the petty cash while Leo lassies haunt the best restaurants. In love, Piscean mamas need considerable tender loving care and so do sapphic Lions. Who will win out?

Pisces and Virgo—Optimistic and cheerful Pisceans are successful partners for serious lesbian Virgins. This spiritual Fish seems to know exactly what to say and do to give her lambda Virgo the confidence she needs to expand her horizons and go for the gold. In love, both of them know exactly what to do to make the other feel special and sexy. I'm jealous!

Pisces and Libra—Both of these babes bring something of value to any relationship, but at the same time they must compromise on many issues in order to keep the fires stoked and burning. In business, both avoid doing the dirty work. In love, queer Fish find themselves sipping flat champagne and watching the candles flicker out while party-hearty sapphic Libras strut their stuff at every clit club in town. My advice: Change the locks.

Pisces and Scorpio—These two highly sensitive women work and play well together. In business, each one contributes the best of their abilities. Rainbow Fish have a tendency to scatter their talents but lambda Scorps are able to keep them on track. In love,

Pisces are more romantic while Scorps are more passionate. Somehow, though, they manage to find common ground.

Pisces and Sagittarius—In business, the devil-may-care Archer may stray too far afield when paired with the impractical proud Fish. Too much gets lost in the static. In love, sapphic Fish may have her love notes trashed by her Sag sisters' clumsy, unfeeling manner. Lesbian Archers may not have the patience to rein in the ramblings of their Piscean lovergrrls' mind games. Agree to disagree and leave it at that.

Pisces and Capricorn—A Capricorn-Pisces combination has its pros and cons. Capricorn dykes are far too conservative and practical to put up with naive and ditsy pink Pisces in day-to-day business arrangements. In love, however, romantic Pisces gals know how to stir (or is it whip) cool Cap mamas into a frenzy. Watch her peak! Is that a cherry on top?

Pisces and Aquarius—Lavender Fish cannot fathom why Aquarians are so cold and distant. In business, there is little meeting of the minds. Aquarian sisters prefer to be left alone to "do their thing" while Piscean mamas need to know every little detail of their partner's comings and goings. Same situation in love. How long will our dear, queer Fish wait for her marshmallows to be toasted? It depends on if her Aquarian lovergrrl remembered to feed the fire.

Pisces and Pisces—When two Piscean mamas get together it will be a trip to the moon on gossamer wings. In business, nothing gets done because both are trying to redecorate the office in a lovely shade of lavender. In love, they may be so intertwined that they have no time to do any food shopping. But who cares as long as you can order in?

famous pisceans: one a day

Cindy Crawford	model	February 20
Anaïs Nin	writer	February 21
Drew Barrymore	actor	February 22
Peter Fonda	actor	February 23
Edward James Olmos	actor	February 24
Sally Jessy Raphael	talk-show host	February 25
Fats Domino	singer	February 26
Elizabeth Taylor	actor	February 27
Bernadette Peters	performer	February 28
Dinah Shore	singer	February 29
Alberta Hunter	singer	March 1
Naomi Jones	adventurer	March 2
Jackie Joyner-Kersee	athlete	March 3
Chastity Bono	activist	March 4
Rosa Luxembourg	revolutionary	March 5
Ann Curtis	athlete	March 6
Janet Gutherie	autoracer	March 7
Cyd Charisse	dancer	March 8
Raul Julia	actor	March 9
Harriet Tubman	activist	March 10
Dorothy Schiff	publisher	March 11
Liza Minnelli	performer	March 12
Neil Sedaka	lyricist, singer	March 13
Diane Arbus	photographer	March 14
Ruth Bader Ginsburg	Supreme Court Justice	March 15
Jerry Lewis	comedian	March 16
Nat King Cole	singer	March 17
Bonnie Blair	athlete	March 18
Glenn Close	actor	March 19
Henrik Ibsen	playwright	March 20

women born on the cusp

Those born between March 17 and March 23 tend to have a combination of Pisces and Aries attributes.

The blending of the last sign of the zodiac (Pisces) with the first (Aries) is a study in contrasts. Aries gals are fairly basic while sapphic Fish need more than just food and shelter to feel complete and whole. Aries rules the head while Pisces rules the feet. So what the heck goes on in between?

The Piscean Ram strives for understanding and intellectual compatibility. They possess extraordinary brain power and are able to conceptualize, implement and launch even the most difficult and detailed projects successfully. Her Piscean influences give her great creativity, intuition and empathy while her Aries influences provide the oomph and persevering followthrough. It is quite a successful combination. There are times though that this enthusiastic and fascinating sister may not always be as logical as one would expect, so check the phases of the moon before you ask her for advice.

Ever the girl scout, she is loyal, helpful, tactful and clean. You'll love her in her uniform with all her little merit badges. But don't for a minute think that this girl is easy pickings. Think of her as a bucking bronco—difficult to ride, hard to rope and almost impossible to hog-tie. Well, I suppose the more difficult the task, the sweeter the success.

Astrology: It's Not Just About People ✳

There are all types of astrological analyses. Sure, people have horoscopes, but so do buildings, countries, corporations, events and even pets. (Drive yourself crazy with an Aries cat, who will never, ever listen to you and will happily chew up your underwear and vomit it up on your pillow.) Anything that happens, at a certain date, time and place is fair game for the astrological gristmill. Those of you with little to do on a Friday night might peruse the chart of the incorporation of IBM or the christening of the *Titanic* or the 1906 San Francisco earthquake or the June 1969 Stonewall Rebellion, which, incidentally, is fully analyzed in this chapter.

The Stonewall Rebellion astrological examination demonstrates how houses, planets, signs and aspects in the chart of that night all piece together in a full and glorious panorama of activity. The planetary transits and their influences on our behaviors caused events to unfold and set the entire course of action . . . absolutely, obviously and thankfully.

stonewall Horoscope

when the paddy wagon pulled up, the mood turned more somber. And it turned sullen when the police officers started to emerge from stonewall with prisoners in tow. . . . All sensed something unusual in the air, all felt a kind of tensed expectancy.
—Martin Duberman, *stonewall* (plume press, 1994)

Astrologers are often consulted to give proper perspective and intelligent illumination to certain major events. For those of us

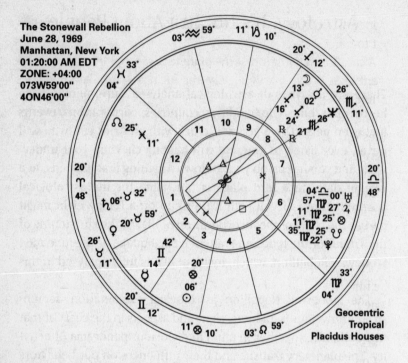

The Stonewall Rebellion
June 28, 1969
Manhattan, New York
01:20:00 AM EDT
ZONE: +04:00
073W59'00"
40N46'00"

Geocentric
Tropical
Placidus Houses

who enjoy a little twenty-twenty hindsight, I modestly offer an
astrological analysis of the events at the Stonewall Rebellion in
1969. I, for one, believe that the planets set the whole thing in
motion.

On June 28, 1969, at approximately 1:20 A.M., an unexpected
police raid was carried out at a bar in Greenwich Village, New
York City. In the past, the patrons would submit to whatever hu-
miliations the police would dole out, but on that particular night,
something happened and enough was enough. The riots lasted
five days and ultimately launched the Gay and Lesbian liberation
movement. Was it the drinks? Was it the music? Was it the company? Or was it the planets? What was it that night that made the

Stonewall riots the event it was and the turning point it turned out to be?

A careful examination of the planetary chart at the time of the event reveals that astrologically, the night was primed for revolution.

The sun, which changes signs about every thirty-two days and rules our life's ambitions and true personalities, was in sentimental and sensitive Cancer that night. It was quite true that emotions were running exceptionally high during that period. (Judy Garland's funeral was held the day before in New York City, and many in the community were devastated by her death.)

The moon, which changes signs about every two days and rules our emotional reaction state, landed in Sagittarius on June 28. Mars, the planet of action and aggression was also in Sag at the time. Rebellious Sagittarius. Poke in the eye Sagittarius. Need I say more? Not only does this particular sign not listen to authority, but it absolutely revels in that wonderful type of "up yours" attitude.

Contemplative Mercury, which was in quick-thinking, quick-acting Gemini, contributed to the highly charged energy, and Venus, the planet of love, was in stubborn Taurus. Taurus the Bull will not be put aside when it is finally pushed to the limit of its patience.

The Ascendant (the First House), which rules first impressions and beginnings of things, was in fiery, no-holds-barred Aries. Aries is the steamroller sign. You can never say no to an Aries.

The MidHeaven (the Tenth House), which is in the highest spot in the sky at that time of night, was in Capricorn. The MidHeaven indicates where we are going and at what speed. It indicates our status in the community and our ultimate goal in life. Capricorn is a sign that experiences difficult beginnings but learns from mistakes and hardship to reach highly successful results. Capricorn also knows how to gain the long-term advantage, what to do and how to do it. It is also one of those unstoppable cardinal signs once it gets going. The old Goat knows just how far to push without getting totally squashed. Hmmmm.

So what do we have so far? Highly charged emotions coupled with an "in your face, don't even try to hold me back" attitude just waiting for justification to act.

The true beauty of astrological analysis is the interaction between the planets, called *aspects.* Aspects cause the energy to take off in one direction or another. It's what gives us our oomph and eventual tri-oomphs. The planetary oomphs that night were fairly dramatic. Here are just a few of them:

The sun had a pleasant aspect to Saturn. Saturn can be a hard taskmaster, but when it "sextiles" the sun, one can experience a terrific learning experience. It can also set things in their proper direction. Stonewall set the entire gay movement in the right direction and there was no turning back. In addition, the sun had a difficult faceoff with explosive and unpredictable Uranus. Who we want to be becomes open to sudden, unexpected changes. We are not pretty during this time. We don't sit back and shut up.

Mercury and the moon didn't see eye to eye—emotions and logical thoughts were not in sync. We do what we are compelled to do, rather than what is most prudent (or most respectful). Tough!

Mars gives us the energy and impetus to act. It had quite a few planetary tête-à-tête aspects that night and, with the exception of delusional Neptune, they were all good. Action produces lucky (Jupiter) and unexpected (Uranus) results. Need I point out that Mars was sitting in the area of the horoscope that affects sex and deep psychological revelations? *Very* interesting. Lie down and tell me about it. . . .

The planet that probably set the whole affair on the map is

volcanic Pluto. Pluto was having some major interactions with others planets that night: (1) Pluto conjunct Uranus and Jupiter—unexpected major transformations that prove initially explosive but ultimately very lucky; (2) Pluto sextile Neptune—we are not sure what to expect and throughout we are almost in a fog, but whatever happens will be big, big, big; (3) Pluto square both the moon and Mercury—we are allowing emotions and ideas to cause some major changes in the current landscape; (4) Pluto trine Venus—expect big and beautiful upheavals. Pluto is unleashed personal power and major transformative change. There is no turning back with this planet. It erupts and changes the landscape. That night, it changed the landscape forever.

Some hack writer once wrote, "[It is] not in the stars but in ourselves that we are underlings." I must disagree. Were it not for the stars that warm June night, who knows what type of life we would be leading today. I shudder to think.

Index

238 ✳ index

O'Keeffe, Georgia, 161
Olmos, Edward James, 227
Onassis, Jacqueline, 109
"on the cusp," 16
opposition aspects, 20
Orwell, George, 92
Owens, Jesse, 127
Ozick, Cynthia, 41

Paglia, Camille, 41
Parker, Dorothy, 109
Parton, Dolly, 111, 190, 194
Pavarotti, Luciano, 143
Perón, Eva, 58
Perrine, Valerie, 127
Peters, Bernadette, 227
Pfeiffer, Michelle, 58
Piaf, Edith, 178
Piscean Age, 214
Pisces, Pisceans, 13, 16, 213–28
    in career and work, 215–16
    communication style of, 221
    cusp of Aquarius and, 212
    cusp of Aries and, 228
    family and parents of, 220
    famous, 227
    friends of, 219
    general personality and first impressions of,
        214–15
    health and fitness of, 221–22
    home of, 217–18
    in love, sex and relationships, 218–19
    money and, 216–17
    in relationships with other signs, 40, 57, 74, 91,
        108, 126, 142, 160, 177, 193, 210, 223–26
    secrets and fears of, 222
    vital statistics of, 213
    weaknesses of, 223
Pitt, Brad, 178
planet areas of dominance, 17, 19
Plath, Sylvia, 161
Plato, 19
Plummer, Christopher, 178
Pollux, 61
Porter, Cole, 75
Post, Emily, 143
Principal, Victoria, 194

Quayle, Marilyn, 109

Rand, Ayn, 206, 211
Raphael, Sally Jessy, 227
Reagan, Nancy, 92
Reddy, Helen, 161
Redford, Robert, 109
Redgrave, Vanessa, 211
Ride, Sally, 75
Rigg, Diana, 92
Ringwald, Molly, 211
Ripken, Cal, Jr., 127
Rivera, Chita, 211
Rogers, Ginger, 92

Rogers, Roy, 161
Ronstadt, Linda, 92
Roosevelt, Eleanor, 132, 139, 143
Ross, Betsy, 194
Rossellini, Isabella, 75
Rudolph, Wilma, 92
Russell, Lillian, 178
Russell, Rosalind, 75

Sade, Marquis de, 75
Sagittarius, Sagittarians, 13, 16, 163–79
    in career and work, 165–66
    communication style of, 170–71
    cusp of Capricorn and, 178
    cusp of Scorpio and, 162
    family and parents of, 170
    famous, 178
    friends of, 169
    general personality and first impressions of,
        164–65
    health and fitness of, 171–72
    home of, 167–68
    in love, sex and relationships, 168–69
    money and, 167
    in relationships with other signs, 39, 57, 75,
        90, 107, 126, 141, 159–60, 174–77, 192–93, 209,
        226
    secrets and fears of, 172–73
    vital statistics of, 163
    weaknesses of, 173
Saliers, Emily, 92
Sarandon, Susan, 143
Saturn, 19, 21
Saturn Return, 21–23
Schiff, Dorothy, 227
Scorpio, Scorpios, 13, 16, 145–62
    in career and work, 147–49
    communication style of, 154–55
    cusp of Libra and, 144
    cusp of Sagittarius and, 162
    family and parents of, 153–54
    famous, 161
    friends of, 152–53
    general personality and first impressions of,
        146–47
    health and fitness of, 155
    home of, 150–51
    in love, sex and relationships, 151–52
    money and, 149–50
    in relationships with other signs, 39, 56–57, 73, 90,
        107, 126, 141, 157–60, 176, 192, 209, 225–26
    secrets and fears of, 156
    vital statistics of, 145
    weaknesses of, 156–57
Sedaka, Neil, 227
Seles, Monica, 178
Semele, 130
Serling, Rod, 194
sextile aspects, 20
Sheedy, Ally, 75
Shields, Brooke, 75
Shore, Dinah, 227